The Learning Organization

ACKNOWLEDGEMENTS

This publication was developed by Scitech Educational in partnership with NEBS Management.

Project management:	Diana Thomas (NEBS Management)
	Don McLeod (Scitech Educational)
Series editor:	Darren O'Conor
Authors:	Phil Wilson and Darren O'Conor

Dossier 04: The Learning Organization

A Scitech Educational publication

Distributed by Scitech-DIOL

ISBN 0 948672 82 X

Published by:
Scitech Educational Ltd
15 – 17 The St John Business Centre
St Peter's Road
Margate
Kent CT9 1TE
United Kingdom

Tel:	+44 (0)1843 234741
Fax:	+44 (0)1843 231485
Website:	www.universal-manager.co.uk
	www.scitechdiol.co.uk

CONTENTS

THE LEARNING ORGANIZATION

THE UNIVERSAL MANAGER SERIES

Books

01 Risk Management
02 Delivering Successful Projects
03 Planning and Controlling Projects
04 The Learning Organization
05 Managing for Knowledge
06 Obtaining and Retaining Customers
07 Human Resource Planning
08 Business Planning
09 Financial Performance
10 Managing Quality
11 Business Relationships
12 Managing for High Performance
13 Managing Harmoniously
14 21st Century Communication
15 Managing for Sustainability

Computer-based Resources

Management Assignments (CD-ROM)
Personal Development Planning Toolkit
      (at www.universal-manager.co.uk)
Learning Styles Toolkit
      (at www.universal-manager.co.uk)

PREFACE

In the early 1990s, at a time of great turbulence for many economies, the learning organization concept caught the imagination of managers all over the world. Initial popularity had something to do with its revisionist approach to learning — forget about MBAs and off-the-job training courses, genuine learning happens every day at the 'sharp end'. For Western governments and organizations, worried about future competitiveness but cautious about spending, this message was a powerful one. Of course it is a dramatic simplification of true learning organization theory, but like most other products, management ideas thrive on the one sentence pitch. While the originators explore facets of 'double loop learning' and 'personal mastery', the marketplace hears:

> *Faster learning = greater competitiveness*
>
> and
>
> *Maximized learning = greater efficiency.*

Ten years further on, the concept might reasonably be described as immature — certainly in the UK it would be difficult to compile a long list of organizations which have fully embraced and benefited from it. In more recent management thinking on topics like knowledge management and Neuro-Linguistic Programming, and in quality standards such as Investors in People and the Business Excellence Model, the influence of learning organization theory can be traced. Many of its insights, startling in the original, are now accepted wisdom, but at least some of the attraction lies in how difficult it is to attain.

This dossier will be equally useful to learners who are new to the concept, and to managers with experience of implementing it. Starting with an explanation of the theory and its origins, we move on to examine how it might work in organizations, its impact, practice and requirements. Along the way *The Learning Organization* surveys current learning practices in both public and private sectors, and provides guidance on managing learning in the workplace effectively.

As well as providing a wealth of information for the general reader, *The Learning Organization* will support candidates working towards the NEBS Management Diploma and the Management S/NVQ at Level 4.

If you are working towards either qualification, your approved centre will provide guidance on how your study of *The Learning Organization* fits in with the overall programme. Appendix 3 of this dossier contains information about the NEBS Management Diploma.

6

LEARNING PROFILE

Topics included in this dossier are listed below. Use them to make a quick judgement about the level of your current knowledge and understanding, and to highlight the sections of the dossier which will be most useful to you.

KEY Low	You have never or not recently studied this topic, nor recently applied the concepts at work.
Mid	You have a broad understanding of the concepts or some experience of working with them, but are not confident about your current level of knowledge.
High	You are familiar with the concepts and their theoretical underpinning. You could confidently apply the concepts in any work context.

	Low	Mid	High
(1) What is a Learning Organization?			
☛ The meaning of the term 'learning organization'	❏	❏	❏
☛ Key thinkers on organizational learning: Senge, Argyris, Schön	❏	❏	❏
(2) Can Organizations Learn?			
☛ The evolution of learning theory (individual)	❏	❏	❏
☛ Theories of intelligence including multiple intelligences and emotional intelligence, and their relevance to the workplace	❏	❏	❏
☛ Strategies for collective learning	❏	❏	❏
(3) The Strategic Impact of Learning			
☛ How may learning affect the way an organization performs?	❏	❏	❏
☛ The benefits of the learning organization	❏	❏	❏
☛ Demonstrating the impact of organizational learning, including the Kirkpatrick and Resource-based HRD models	❏	❏	❏
☛ What does a learning organization look like?	❏	❏	❏
☛ The Investors in People Standard	❏	❏	❏
(4) Learning Needs Analysis			
☛ The value of needs analysis	❏	❏	❏
☛ Approaches to needs analysis including the competency-based approach	❏	❏	❏
(5) Developing a Learning Culture			
☛ What is organizational culture?	❏	❏	❏
☛ How culture can foster organizational learning	❏	❏	❏
☛ Strategies for achieving a learning culture	❏	❏	❏
☛ The significance of direction, leadership, development and review processes in building a learning culture	❏	❏	❏
(6) Current Practice in Learning and Development			
☛ Continuing Professional Development and Self Managed Learning	❏	❏	❏
☛ Traditional methods; on-job, off-job, short course provision	❏	❏	❏
☛ Non-traditional methods; open, distance and computer-based learning	❏	❏	❏
☛ Action learning	❏	❏	❏
☛ Maximizing experience and effort via knowledge transfer, competitive intelligence, performance review, coaching and mentoring	❏	❏	❏

04-1 WHAT IS A 'LEARNING ORGANIZATION'?

04-1 WHAT IS A 'LEARNING ORGANIZATION'?

Death and taxes are no longer the only certainties in life; there is now a third certainty — constant change. Today, the most successful organizations are those that not only cope with change but thrive on it, bearing out the words of Charles Darwin:

> *'It is not the strongest of the species nor the most intelligent (which survive) but the ones most responsive to change.'*

In organizations, as in nature, success in a competitive environment comes to those best able to adapt to changes in that environment; evolutionary competition is pitiless, favouring those best able to exploit their environment, and killing off the weak. However, in nature, evolutionary processes are unconscious and blind, whereas in well-functioning learning organizations, intelligent, reasoned responses can be made in order to adapt to the environment and compete within it. The ability to learn is therefore critical to the survival and growth of organizations, or as Ray Stata (CEO of Analog Devices) is quoted in Peter Senge's '*The Fifth Discipline*':

> *'The rate at which an organization learns may become the only sustainable source of competitive advantage.'*

04-1-1 The Concept of the Learning Organization

For reasons which will become evident, it is important to establish what we understand by the term 'learning organization'. To begin with, have a look at the following definitions:

> *'A learning organization is one in which people at all levels, individually and collectively, are continually increasing their capacity to produce results they really care about.'*

(Richard Karash, http://www.learning-org.com)

> *'Organizational learning means the process of improving actions through better knowledge and understanding.'*

(Fiol & Lyles, 'Organizational Learning', *Academy of Management Review*, October 1985.)

'Organizations are seen as learning by encoding inferences from history into routines that guide behaviour.'
(Levitt & March, 1988, 'Organizational Learning', *American Review of Sociology*.)

'Organizational learning is a process of detecting and correcting error.'
(C Argyris, 1977, *Double Loop Learning in Organizations*, HBR.)

'A learning organization is an organization skilled at creating, acquiring and transferring knowledge, and at modifying its behaviour to reflect new knowledge and insights.'
(D Garvin, *Building a Learning Organization*, HBR, July – August 1993.)

PAUSE TO REFLECT

From your reading of the above interpretations, what key characteristics of the learning organization emerge?

Now read on.

From the previous exercise it should have become apparent that, though there are many different ways of describing organizational learning, the essentials remain the same. Some of the key words we picked out of the previous definitions are:

- ☞ *Collective*. The issue of whether groups, particularly large groups, can learn collectively is at the heart of the learning organization concept. We examine this issue in Section 04-2 of this dossier.
- ☞ *Improving*. The purpose of work-based learning is to improve performance, but in most organizations this means that the impact of learning on performance needs to measured. Not only is this difficult to do, but it can create a tension between the view that learning is a lifelong process, and the need for results in the here and now.
- ☞ *Knowledge and understanding*. Skills underpinned by knowledge and understanding is the UK definition of competence. This is important because it begins to blur traditional divisions between managers who think and workers who do. In today's workplace, there are very few mechanical jobs.

Office Shredder!

☛ *History*. Organizational history has been seized upon by some as the answer to the dilemma of collective learning. In the same way that, say, Germany and Japan have the 'lessons' of World War II engraved on the national psyche, so too, can organizations learn from significant events in their own history. It's a contention which does, however, beg certain supplementary questions, such as can success teach as well as failure?

☛ *Behaviour*. The true test of learning is behaviour. Individual and organizational learning is undertaken to change behaviour but there are other cultural factors in organizations which may have equal or greater influence on the way people behave.

☛ *Process*. A cynic might feel that 'it's a process, not an event' is what management consultants say when their 'solutions' don't work out. But if it applies to any management idea, the learning organization is the one. In learning organizations, learning is a continuous process, and the pay-off may be gradual and, if the ambition is particularly high, may take a while to pay off.

☛ *Insight*. One of the pay-offs from organizational learning should be enhanced self-awareness, an ability to 'mine' and share important insights from past experience. In this sense, the learning organization shares much common ground with the discipline of knowledge management.

Late 1970s	1980s	1990s	2000
Competitive forces	Total Quality Empowerment Re-engineering	Learning Organization Core Competencies Knowledge Management	The Virtual Organization

This by no means comprehensive survey of developing management theory since the late 1970s is intended to put the idea of the learning organization into context. This is instructive for two reasons:

☛ First, to note that the one common factor linking all of these is competitiveness. The perpetual quest in management research and thinking is to find out what gives certain organizations the edge.

☛ Second, the timing of organizational learning theory is interesting. Its rise roughly coincided with the decline of re-engineering and there is a surprising amount of common ground between the two ideas.

　☛ Both are partly concerned with maximizing resources (with re-engineering the emphasis was on people, finance and physical assets: in the learning organization the resources are intangibles such as experience and knowledge)

　☛ Both insist on a systemic approach to the organization and its problems (re-engineering requires analysis of the whole organization within its environment, before identifying solutions: we shall discuss the learning organization approach to 'systems thinking' later in this section)

12

☞ Both rely on an open mindset (re-engineering urges top management to re-design their organizations from scratch; while learning organization theory encourages us all to be aware of the limiting effects of our 'mental models').

04-1

PAUSE TO REFLECT

Given these striking similarities, why is re-engineering a largely discredited theory while the popularity of the learning organization endures?

Now read on.

It may be to do with the fact that many of the tens of thousands of managers made redundant in the name of re-engineering subsequently went into consultancy, and were hardly disposed to champion the ideas that put them out of work!

Perhaps two slightly more convincing reasons are that:

☞ Re-engineering forgot about people. In striving for the leanest possible organization, many companies dispensed with several thousands of years in accumulated expertise and experience. Once gone, it could not be replaced.
☞ The learning organization concept has been able to adapt to the arrival of subsequent 'hot topics', and is in fact viewed as complementary to many of them:

　☞ *Knowledge management* for instance is an important function within the learning organization
　☞ The act of organizational learning will enable the definition and development of *core competencies*
　☞ Even the *virtual organization* relies on its ability to learn, and utilize that learning in the pursuit of its goals.

04-1-2   Key Thinkers on Organizational Learning

How organizations change in response to changing environments has long been the thrust of research into organizational management — in particular, how do individuals, especially managers, undertake problem-solving processes? In the 1980s Chris Argyris and Donald Schön were at the forefront of this work. Schön, for example, examined the importance of reflective practice and in a lecture commented:

> *'Professionals are called upon to perform tasks for which they have not been educated. . . . Professional practice has at least as much to do with FINDING the problem as with SOLVING the problem.'*

Schön was dissatisfied with the attempts of the US education system to deliver a body of knowledge in which theory and scholarship was over-valued, as he saw it, by comparison with vocational or applied studies. In a lecture to the American Educational Research Association in 1987 (http://educ.queensu.ca/russellt/schon87.htm) he expressed the wish to see the education system deliver more of what he called 'knowledge-in-action' — thinking in new ways about phenomena and applying experimentation. In turn, he felt this would give rise to 'reflection-on-action' and 'reflection-in-action' which Schön felt was key to solving practical problems. These ideas are explored in his influential book *Educating the Reflective Practitioner* (1983).

Whether through persuasiveness or good timing, Schön's ideas have been influential in the workplace and also within the UK education system. Though it cannot be said that applied learning has yet acquired parity with academic education, it is gaining ground, and has been supported since the late 1980s by a series of initiatives such as the development of a framework for National Vocational Qualifications (NVQs).

Argyris' interests covered the same issues, but lay in the field of business and management. His contention was that far too much reliance was placed on managers being right! Given a problem, he argued, managers tend to look for a 'quick fix' — they want to solve the problem, to be rid of it and to move on to the next one. Yet often, the same problems keep returning . . . the 'quick fix' has not produced a lasting solution, and the problems have not gone away. The typical manager, according to Argyris, is conditioned to see only the immediate and superficial nature of the problem and will usually fail to address underlying causes. The application of a second phase to the problem solving process, in which those underlying causes are properly analysed is, in Argyris' view, the only way to break out of the closed orbit of repeated failure.

The double loop learning theory proposed by Argyris and Schön (1974) sets out a 'theory of action' to address the identified conflict or divergence between intention and outcome. In a single loop problem solving process, the root causes of the problem are not examined but action is changed in response to the unsatisfactory outcome. The double loop model aims to break the cycle of recurring problems by ensuring that the problem solver, working with others, examines the root causes.

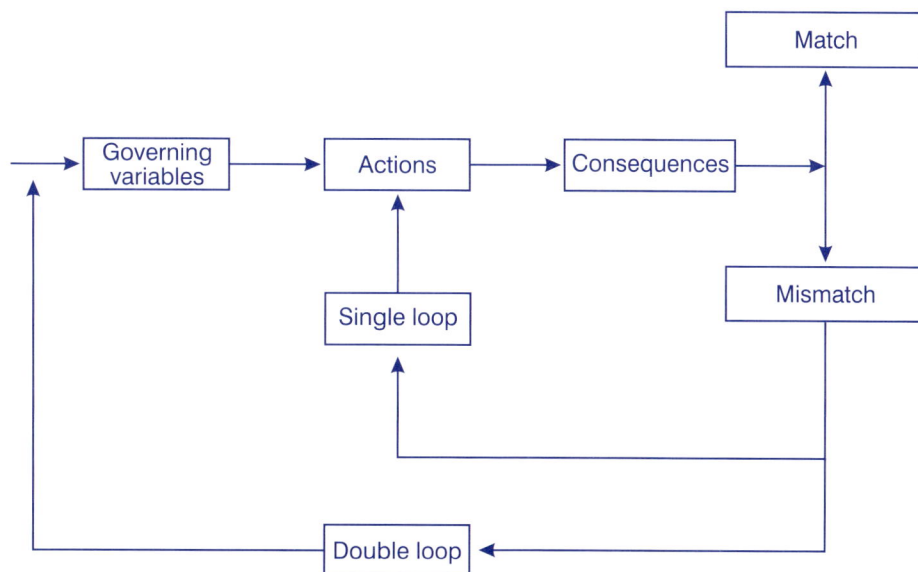

Argyris calls his system of thinking 'Action Science' in which theory is put into practice and thoughts are put into action. He sees group interactions as all-important, and believes that openness and honesty can help to focus on the root causes of problems and help to develop new systems, frameworks and routines. Part of the challenge for organizations is to identify and remove the barriers preventing open and frank exchange, such as vested interest and fear of admitting to mistakes. For more on Argyris' Action Science, see:

www.actionscience.com/actinq.htm

Building on the ideas of Argyris, Schön and others, Peter Senge set out an organizational framework in his 1990 book, *The Fifth Discipline*, subtitled *The Art and Practice of the Learning Organization*, that he believes to be essential for organizations to function effectively in a rapidly changing world. Senge is widely credited with the phrase and concept of the learning organization and it is with his two key works (*The Fifth Discipline* and *The Fifth Discipline Fieldbook*) that most students of the theory begin, and probably end, their work.

The Learning Organization

However, as Senge himself is aware, many readers struggle to put his ideas into practice in the work-place. And where they may succeed in implementing one or two of his ideas, very few have managed to realize the entire framework Senge puts forward. Senge addressed these problems in *The Fifth Discipline Fieldbook* (1994), which builds on the original theory to provide a more practical framework, defined by the book's subtitle — *Strategies and Tools for Building a Learning Organization*.

The essence of Senge's theory of the learning organization is in five interdependent disciplines: four of these (Personal Mastery, Mental Models, Shared Vision and Team Learning) describe individual and group capabilities — these essential or core components are cemented together by what is described as 'Systems Thinking' which is the Fifth Discipline of the book. This overall five-part framework Senge sees as creating an effective environment in which organizational learning and continuous development can thrive.

(1)   *Personal Mastery*

This core discipline relates to individual learning and has two sub-components, first the need to define an individual vision or visions and second an awareness of where you are in relation to the vision. Unlike the short-, medium-, and long-term goals normally considered in organizational management, the visions within Personal Mastery may well take a lifetime to achieve and, in striving towards them, individuals will experience continuous development in their thought processes.

According to Senge, when people enter the 'mind-set' of Personal Mastery and practise it on a daily basis they experience changes in their outlook and thinking; their reasoning and intuitive powers increase; they tend towards becoming systems thinkers, able to perceive connections and relationships between diverse elements in their professional and personal lives.

(2)   *Mental Models*

This discipline refers to the mental processes by which we perceive and interact with the environment around us. Our Mental Models are often formed during our developmental years and may well be based on deeply ingrained assumptions. Clearly, if our Mental Models are flawed, or if they are mis-aligned with the Mental Models of those around us, then communication is likely to be impaired.

www.universal-manager.co.uk

PAUSE TO REFLECT

How might Mental Models constrain organizational performance?

Now read on.

A fixed mindset can be dangerous to any organization and might result in:

- Mistaken assumptions about the nature of the competition (think of how the major oil companies have been outflanked in the UK by retail giants like Tesco and Sainsburys)
- Costly missed opportunities (missing the shift from analogue to digital technology by just one year cost Motorola its position as the world's leading mobile phone company)
- Failure to build on advantages (the major banks in the US and UK have lost a lot of ground over the last 10 to 15 years — it has taken them a long time to appreciate what innovators like FirstDirect grasped, that customers want banking on their own terms).

Chris Argyris' work, and that of his colleagues at Harvard University, on which this aspect of Senge's work is based, suggests that much of our reasoning is based on flawed Mental Models. As a result, when we are re-confronted by a similar problem, rather than learning from our mistakes, we tend to enter the same loop of behaviour and repeat the same mistakes over and over again. By learning to see the flaws in our Mental Models, Argyris believes that we can break out of the single (repeating) loop to create situations in which genuine and lasting progress is made.

(3)   *Shared Vision*

Vision is an important quality in the learning organization. It is central to Personal Mastery and re-occurs in this discipline, where Senge sees the need for an organization to have a vision that is shared by its members. For the vision to be truly shared and held in common, he believes, it is critical that it should be developed collectively and not simply foisted upon the organization by senior executives. By enrolling into the Shared Vision, members of the organization demonstrate participation and commitment, and those who do not or cannot share it are likely to be less productive members of the organization.

The Learning Organization

The dichotomy between vision and reality is what Senge calls 'creative tension'. Recognition of this dichotomy is a type of gap analysis that will focus on the learning needs of the organization and help to propel the organization towards its shared 'picture of the future'.

(4)   *Team Learning*

Senge differentiates between team learning and team building — team building is seen as improving communication, working better together and strengthening relationships. Team learning is defined by Senge as:

> *'. . . the process of aligning and developing the capacity of a team to create the results its members truly desire. It builds on the discipline of developing Shared Vision. It also builds on Personal Mastery, for talented teams are made up of talented individuals.'*

But, how to achieve this elusive goal? The most important feature of team learning is dialogue, and this is enhanced by team members working effectively as a group, sharing understanding, having mutual respect and working with a group leader who holds the threads of the team's dialogue together. To expect all teams to function well and work together as a learning team is naïve, according to Senge. Team members take time to develop proper relationships and, until team members accept their roles within the team, progress may be slow. Ideally, once the team is optimized, then its productivity should greatly exceed the sum of the productivity of individual members — and once this state is achieved, team learning can begin in earnest so that, through dialogue, the group develops new and better ways of working.

(5)   *Systems Thinking*

This is the fifth discipline, and the one which bonds together the other four distinct elements in the learning organization framework. Typically when studying organizations and problems within organizations, a process of reductionism is applied in which, for ease and clarity, the whole is broken into its constituent parts. Such methodology can, however, give misleading results; this is because insufficient consideration is given to the complex interactions and interrelationships of the parts. In other words, the complexities of organizational systems cannot be properly understood by simply knowing what each part is doing. What is needed, is an understanding of both the parts and the whole — systems thinkers are those people who have appropriate mental capacities to see both organizational minutiae and also 'the big picture'.

Senge describes systems thinking as:

'. . . a shift of mind from seeing parts to seeing wholes; from seeing people as helpless reactors to seeing them as active participants in shaping their reality; and from reacting to the present to creating the future.'

Throughout the remainder of this dossier we will explore recent applications and extenions of Senge's original concept. But it is interesting to note at this stage that no one has significantly added to the model outlined in *The Fifth Discipline* since its publication. The numerous publications and presentations on the subject since have concentrated on refining, challenging or applying the model and it would be fair to say that in the field of organizational learning, Senge's five disciplines remain definitive.

CASE STUDY: GUINNESS

Guinness, the Dublin brewer of world repute, foresaw some years ago the likely effects of their transition from a craft-based company to a high-technology company. They made a conscious decision to become a Learning Organisation and by using LO methods have managed to retrain, up-skill and redeploy many employees into new technology areas. The company now produces a high volume, consistent product using far fewer staff. John Findlater, Training and Development Manager, commenting on twenty years of continuous change at an ECLO conference in 1997, said:

' For over 200 years the Guinness brewery at St. James' Gate Dublin has been a labour intensive traditional brewery in which the workers were part of a family group living in the neighbourhood and using manual skills handed down from father to son. In the last 20 years the brewery has made a rapid transition by investing 250 million ECU in new technology to become a world leader in brewing technology. Imagine what it has been like for those craftsmen and operators who had traditional skills. The changes they are facing are massive. The skills of brewing were taken literally out of their hands as they faced the turmoil of adapting to new technology.'

www.eclo.com/conferences/1997/a02.htm

Key to Guinness' success is what Findlater describes as 'relentless communication' — this is necessary because, as he says, 'all the answers are on the site'.

04-2 CAN ORGANIZATIONS LEARN?

04-2

04-2 CAN ORGANIZATIONS LEARN?

Learning theory is something of an academic battleground, fought over by disciplines as various as neurology, psychology, sociology, pedagogy and more recently computer science and multimedia design. In view of the resulting complexity in this field, it is probably not necessary (nor even helpful) for most managers to have an in-depth understanding of the theory of learning.

But three commonly observed trends in organizations today do suggest that an understanding of some of the key principles of learning theory is critical to successful line management:

- After being engineered out of the picture in many organizations, intermediary line management tiers have been reforming over the last five years or so
- The line manager's role is now widely recognized as pivotal in performance management and improvement, at organizational, team and individual levels
- Human resource management increasingly forms part of the generalist manager's role: tasks are likely to include identifying and addressing the team's learning needs.

Recognition of these new or additional functions of the line manager has been slow to dawn, and it is only recently that many large- and medium-sized organizations in the UK have begun to define and implement frameworks of management competence. Even in this commendable undertaking, the importance of learning as a concept and as an act is often addressed only glancingly.

In this section, our intention is to introduce some current and relevant thinking about the way people (and particularly employed adults) learn. We will focus on attempts to understand how different internal and external factors mitigate the impact of learning on individuals, before turning to the topic of how collective learning takes place.

Before we begin, you may find it useful to think about some of your own preconceptions to do with learning. The following activity is designed to help you do this.

ACTION ACTIVITY 1

Before working through the rest of this section, write down brief answers to the following questions about your own experience and attitudes to learning. At the end of the section, you may find it illuminating to revisit your responses and to reconsider them in the light of your study.

04-2

(1)   Think about two or three of the most powerful, effective pieces of learning you have experienced. Why were they so remarkable? What made them work for you? Do your different examples share any common characteristics?

(2)   What in your view are the most important outcomes of (adult) learning activities and processes?

(3)   What factors in your experience tend to inhibit or prevent learning from taking place?

(4)   What qualities would you ascribe to 'a good learner'?

(5) Do you believe that groups of people learn together? If so, how do you think this is possible?

Now read on.

04-2-1 Adult Learning

A convergence of various macro-factors has contributed to making the early twenty first century a fascinating period in the development of adult learning, particularly for the Western economies:

☛ People are living longer, and populations show a general ageing trend

☛ The decline of many traditional industries is arguably matched by the emergence of new ones with very different human resource and skills needs, and increasing reliance on technology

☛ Work-forces are more mobile than ever before, to the extent that it is now possible for the UK's Health Service to recruit entire nursing cohorts from the Philippines

☛ The increasing speed and plurality of communications media ('connectivity') has placed a premium on the currency of information and knowledge.

Against this backdrop, many governments worldwide have promoted the concept of lifelong learning over the last ten years or so. With its echo of Senge's discipline of personal mastery, lifelong learning is intended to solve several problems at once:

☛ *The problem of diminishing state funding for education.* If they accept the need to develop throughout their lives, people are more likely to take personal responsibility for their development, to the extent of investing financially in learning that might previously have been paid for by the state.

☛ *The problems of higher unemployment and declining demand for 'traditional skills'.* A work-force committed to lifelong learning will be equipped to learn new skills and knowledge (and be more adept at identifying portable competences).

www.universal-manager.co.uk

☞ *The problems of an ageing population and therefore an ageing work-force*. Pure lifelong learning means that everybody learns all the time regardless of age or place within an organizational hierarchy. Retirement from work does not equate to 'leaving school' — lifelong learning is about retaining an active and enquiring mind as long as we live.

In the UK, we see signs of the national shift to lifelong learning in, for instance, the increasingly flexible access and delivery policies of higher and further education, and in the implementation of the National Vocational Qualification framework, intended to supply standards for progression in all sectors of industry. Both of these developments are part of a wider change to the way learning is delivered, and they address some of the barriers that have been identified as preventing many adults from benefiting from learning.

04-2

PAUSE TO REFLECT

Can you think of specific barriers that have prevented you, or colleagues, benefiting from learning?

Now read on.

It is perhaps most useful to define two categories of barrier: those which prevent someone taking up learning in the first place, and those which prevent them from obtaining real benefit once engaged in some form of learning. (For the time-being we treat learning in its more conventional sense of training or education activities.)

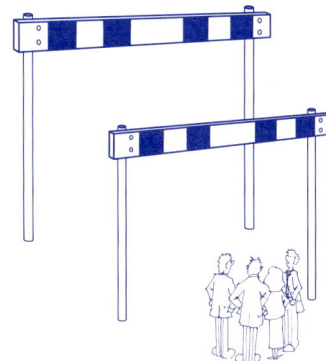

(1)   *Barriers to take-up*

☞ *Lack of awareness*. Without a knowledge of what learning provision is available and suitable for them, people will not move from 'square one'. We see this for instance in many parts of the construction industry, where between statutory health and safety training and development for junior managers, there is often no organized learning or development — employers and employees alike rarely consider it necessary.

☞ *Lack of desire*. Typically, and counter to the principles of lifelong learning, the older we get and the further we travel within the organizational hierarchy, the weaker our motivation to learn becomes. Many adults, scarred by unhappy experiences of school education, have a strong aversion to learning.

☞ *Lack of suitable provision.* In fact, it would be quite unusual to identify learning needs not addressed in some way by available learning provision. But the form or arrangement of available provision can often prevent take-up of learning: for instance, many training and development activities still require people to attend daytime events, away from the work-place. For many employers, particularly small and medium-sized enterprises, this is the least desirable way of having their employees learn new skills or knowledge.

☞ *Cost.* It is a truism that when budgets are tight, human resourcing is often the first part of an organization to feel the effects — and this includes investment in learning and development. Significant professional learning will often cost £'000s and few individuals are able or willing to make that order of investment. Part of the reason that cost can inhibit learning is that few of us perceive it as priority to rank alongside, say, buying a new car, saving for a holiday or even trading up on the housing market. Many organizations and individuals have difficulty comparing the expected benefits of learning with the potential costs; hence a realistic value of learning is often elusive.

☞ *Inconvenience.* This barrier may take all sorts of forms: perhaps the learning activity involves travel over a considerable distance, it may be difficult for the learner to fit in alongside family commitments, or it may require the learner to use resources (such as computer equipment) which are difficult for the learner to obtain.

This has by no means been an exhaustive discussion of the barriers preventing learning take-up, you may be able to think of additional barriers to address in the following activity.

ACTIVITY 2

How might your organization, and you as a line manager, address the barriers preventing people from taking up learning? We list five significant barriers below, but you may be able to identify others which need to be (or are being) removed in your own workplace.

(1)   Lack of awareness

(2)   Lack of desire

(3)   Lack of suitable provision

(4)   Cost

(5)   Inconvenience

(6)

(7)

(8)

Compare your responses with our commentary in Appendix 1.

Assuming the barriers preventing take-up are removed or insignificant, even after enrolling for learning there are several obstacles which may prevent the learner deriving genuine benefit. Failure to deal with this second class of barrier may result in drop-out from learning programmes, low commitment to learning as it happens, or failure to apply new skills and knowledge in the work-place. Again we summarize five commonly encountered barriers below, but there are many others which can reduce the positive impact of learning.

(2) *Barriers to effective learning*

☛ *Inappropriate method*. A significant aspect of current learning theory is the concept of 'learning styles'. Working from an assumption that people respond to different learning methods in different ways, various thinkers have proposed learning style models to help match people to their optimum learning method. Although there is limited evidence of success with any specific model of learning styles, the underlying principle — that learning success depends in part upon the suitability of the method for the individual learner — is now widely accepted. We will return to this point later with a discussion of Kolb's influential model of learning styles.

☛ *Inappropriate level*. It may appear common sense that learners will be turned off by subject matter which is either too easy (or presented in a patronizing manner) or too complex for their current abilities. Yet how many learning programmes make a genuine attempt to identify the current level of skills, experience or knowledge the learner has, and then to tailor delivery so that it enables the learner to make incremental progress?

☛ *Insufficient relevance*. If learning should be designed to match the learner's level, it should also be directly relevant to their identified need. Again, this may seem obvious, but it is very common for general solutions to be offered for very precise problems. An example is the employer who sends all managers on a project management course (regardless of previous experience and qualifications) when the specific need was for improvement in the management of relationships with clients and sub-contractors. A good project management course would address those issues, but only alongside a lot of other, possibly irrelevant content.

☞ *Lack of support*. Support for adult learning can take many forms: it might be a case of getting grandparents to look after the children occasionally; some organizations offer study leave to employees; and support could also be considered in terms of resources such as access to a computer or internet facility. Any of these factors could affect the learner's experience positively, but for work-based learning, the most influential factor is undoubtedly the support of the line manager. By helping to plan and arrange learning, by asking how it's going, and by reviewing outcomes, line managers can make employees' learning truly effective. Conversely, if line managers stay remote from the learning of their team, often this alone can render the process ineffective.

04-2

☞ *Lack of tangible result*. It is human nature in any endeavour to want to see some reward for our efforts — and most of us have a diminishing supply of patience. It is important therefore that learning is designed to allow its participants to experience tangible results as early as possible. For work-based learning this means introducing practical activity at an early stage, and encouraging learners to transfer new skills and knowledge (and reflect on the transfer of) to their workroles. For line managers, the importance of feedback and recognition is emphasized again.

ACTION **ACTIVITY 3**

This is similar to the previous activity. This time we want you to consider how your organization, and you as a line manager, might address the barriers inhibiting effective learning. We list our five barriers below, but you may be able to identify others which need to be (or are being) removed in your own workplace.

(1)   Inappropriate method

(2)   Inappropriate level

(3)   Insufficient relevance

(4)   Lack of support

(5)   Lack of tangible result

(6)

(7)

(8)

Compare your responses with our commentary in Appendix 1.

Much of the foregoing is grounded in some widely accepted principles of learning theory. We have already stated that few managers need to become experts in this field. But for those with a specific interest in ideas about how we learn, a very brief overview of some of the most influential theories might be useful.

(1)   Characteristics of Adults as Learners (CAL)

CAL is a model developed by K P Cross (1981) and has direct relevance to the principle of lifelong learning. Cross identifies two main variables influencing receptiveness to learning: personal and situational characteristics.

Personal characteristics include ageing, life phases (such as marriage, having children, etc.) and developmental stages (e.g. job changing, retirement). Each characteristic affects lifelong learning in different ways. Ageing, for instance, results in the deterioration of certain sensory-motor abilities (e.g. eyesight, hearing, reaction time) while intelligence abilities (e.g. decision-making skills, reasoning, vocabulary) tend to improve.

Situational characteristics describe the arrangement of the learning itself: whether it is part-time or full-time learning, who is providing it, where the learning takes place, and so on. They also relate to the context in which the learning is being undertaken: whether it is compulsory or voluntary for instance.

Cross articulates four important principles of adult learning:

- It should capitalize on the experience of participants
- It should adapt to the age limitations of the participants
- It should challenge participants to progress to increasingly advanced stages of personal development
- It should offer as much choice as possible in the availability and organization of learning.

www.universal-manager.co.uk

(2)   Behaviourist versus Constructivist Theory

The architect of constructivist theory was Bruner (1966, 1986, 1990). Its central premise was initially a reaction to the prevailing behaviourist view of learning which contended that behaviour is shaped by its consequences, and can thus be conditioned by a pattern or reinforcement (or reward) and correction (or punishment).

04-2

Constructivists believe that learning is an active process in which learners construct new ideas or concepts based upon their current/past knowledge. Behaviourist learning design maps out the entire learning domain and devises step by step programmes for learning — it therefore puts the instructor at the centre of the process. By contrast, the constructivist approach is 'learner-centred.' The learner selects and transforms information, constructs hypotheses, and makes decisions. The aim is to encourage learners to experiment and go beyond the information given — instructors should try and encourage students to discover principles by themselves, either by engaging them in an active dialogue or by translating information to be learned into a format appropriate to the learner's current state of understanding.

PAUSE TO REFLECT

Think about the most recent learning activities you have undertaken. Which approaches do you feel they tended towards: behaviourist or constructivist?

Now read on.

Most learning on offer to adults usually adopts the behaviourist approach: short courses, seminars, qualification programmes, and demonstrations all tend to (attempt to) deliver a pre-determined and limited body of knowledge, or set of competences.

By incorporating optional units or modules, some programmes do offer a degree of choice, and there are many forms of learning (such as open learning) which also leave the timing, order and pace up to the student. However, truly constructivist learning, which allows the learner to make their own way through a many-layered 'domain' is rare outside full-time higher education. Computer-based learning (which we look at in Section 04-6-3) has the potential to allow learners the flexibility to construct their own programmes, but at present the best examples carry a high price tag.

(3)   Gagné's Conditions of Learning

The learning theorist Robert Gagné has been very influential on the design of computer-based learning materials. He has an essentially behaviourist belief that the process of instruction should be based on a detailed analysis of the skills required by learners, and that discrete components of instruction should then be designed around a particular task.

Gagné (1977) identifies five main outcomes from the learning process:

☛   Verbal information — in which the respondent is able to restate material that has been previously learned

☛   Intellectual skills — this is subdivided into five further sub-categories: concrete concepts, defined concepts, discriminations, rules and higher order rules — these are used in mental manipulations of information/ knowledge

☛   Cognitive strategies — these guide an individual's learning, thinking and feeling

☛   Attitudes — defining one's outlooks

☛   Motor skills — defining one's physical capabilities.

Gagné is perhaps best known for his nine stage process of instruction, which we summarize below:

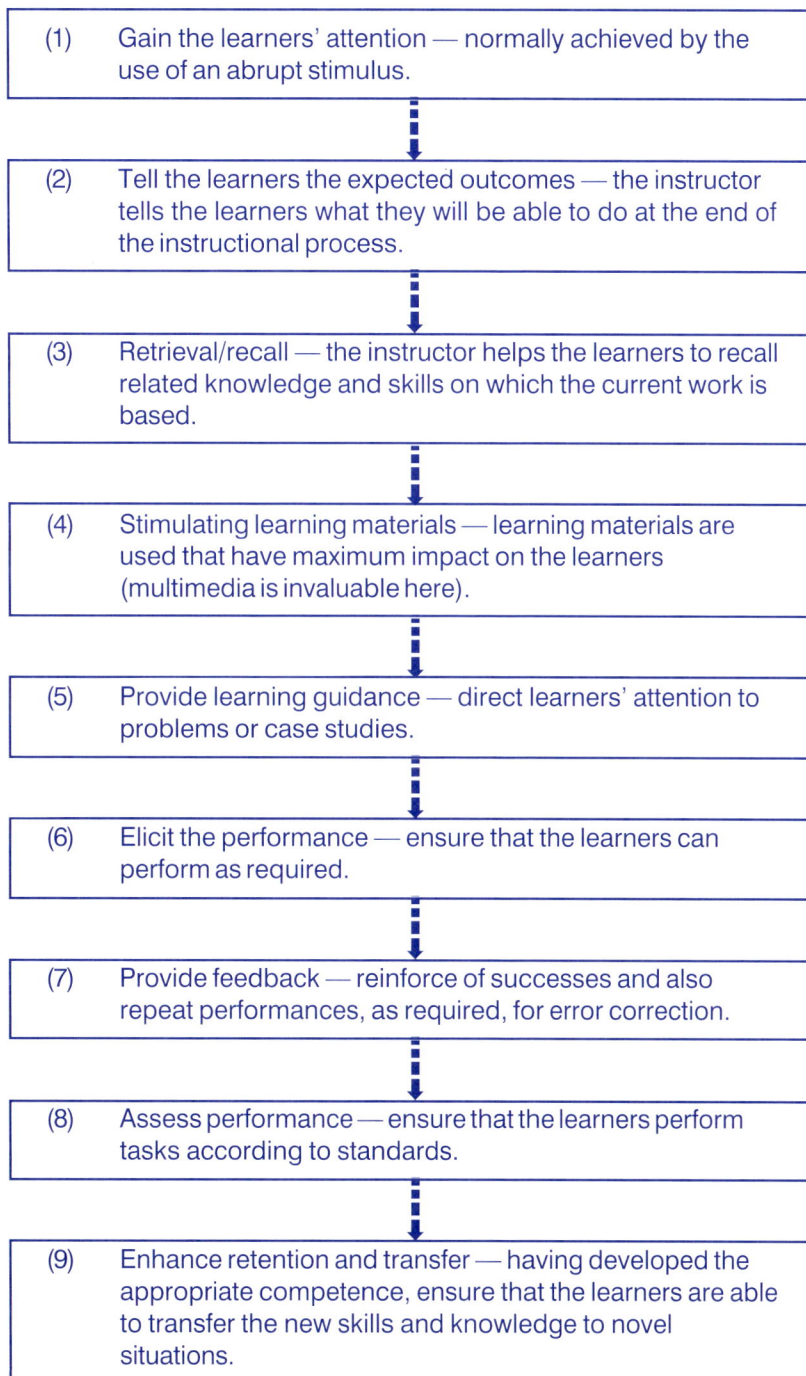

(1)	Gain the learners' attention — normally achieved by the use of an abrupt stimulus.

↓

(2)	Tell the learners the expected outcomes — the instructor tells the learners what they will be able to do at the end of the instructional process.

↓

(3)	Retrieval/recall — the instructor helps the learners to recall related knowledge and skills on which the current work is based.

↓

(4)	Stimulating learning materials — learning materials are used that have maximum impact on the learners (multimedia is invaluable here).

↓

(5)	Provide learning guidance — direct learners' attention to problems or case studies.

↓

(6)	Elicit the performance — ensure that the learners can perform as required.

↓

(7)	Provide feedback — reinforce of successes and also repeat performances, as required, for error correction.

↓

(8)	Assess performance — ensure that the learners perform tasks according to standards.

↓

(9)	Enhance retention and transfer — having developed the appropriate competence, ensure that the learners are able to transfer the new skills and knowledge to novel situations.

(4)   Experiential Learning

Carl Rogers (1994) distinguished two types of learning: cognitive (meaningless) and experiential (significant). 'Meaningless' might appear a slightly harsh description of cognitive learning; in fact Rogers implies that this type of learning has no practical significance or application when it is undertaken. He is referring to academic knowledge such as learning vocabulary or multiplication tables. Experiential learning deals with applied knowledge such as learning about engines in order to repair a car. Key to the distinction is that experiential learning addresses the needs and wants of the learner.

Rogers advocates experiential learning because of its qualities of personal involvement, self-initiation and self-evaluation, and because of the more lasting effect he believes it has compared with cognitive learning. He equates experiential learning to personal change and growth. Some essential principles of the theory of experiential learning are that:

- Significant learning takes place when the subject matter is relevant to the personal interests of the student
- Learning which is threatening to the self (e.g. new attitudes or perspectives) is more easily assimilated when external threats are minimized
- Learning proceeds faster when the threat to the self is low
- Self-initiated learning is the most lasting and pervasive.

(5)   Minimalism

The minimalist theory of J M Carroll (1990) is a framework for the design of instruction, especially training materials for computer users. Minimalism builds on constructivist learning theory and suggests that:

- All learning tasks should be meaningful and self-contained activities
- Learners should be given realistic projects as quickly as possible in the learning process
- Instruction should permit self-directed reasoning and improvising by increasing the number of active learning opportunities
- Learning materials (in whatever format) should provide for error recognition and recovery
- Wherever possible, the learning environment should match the practical or actual environment for which the learner is preparing.

(6)   Cognitive and Learning Styles

Cognitive or learning styles refer to the preferred way an individual processes information, i.e. the way an individual assimilates information, remembers it or applies it to problems.

PAUSE TO REFLECT

Are you aware of your own preferred learning style? If you are set the task of learning something new what is your preferred technique? Perhaps you like to read a book, watch a video, take a computer-based module, or engage in one-to-one or group discussions?

04-2

Now read on.

A number of learning styles have been identified over the years. One of the best known theories came from David Kolb (1984). He identifies two separate learning activities: perception and processing. How people best perceive information is dependent on their mental make-up. For example, they may prefer to use concrete experiences such as touching, seeing, hearing and feeling whereas other people may best perceive information in abstract forms, for example using visual or mental conceptual isolation. Perception is primarily to do with the senses, whereas processing information is all about what happens once messages have been received by the brain.

Kolb's model described a cycle of four dimensions of learning:

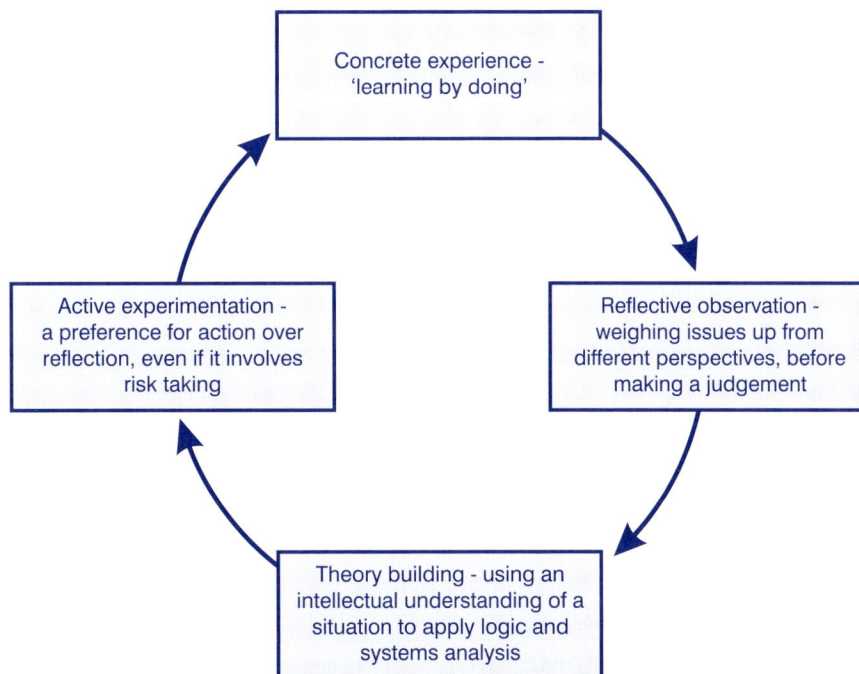

Concrete experience -
'learning by doing'

Reflective observation -
weighing issues up from
different perspectives, before
making a judgement

Theory building - using an
intellectual understanding of a
situation to apply logic and
systems analysis

Active experimentation -
a preference for action over
reflection, even if it involves
risk taking

The model recognizes four principal types or learner:

Type I
Typically 'hands on' — there is a reliance on intuition rather than logic and a tendency to be reliant on other people's analyses. This learner is good at applications, and enjoys putting his or her learning into practice.

Type II
Gathers information, adopts many perspectives and values imagination in finding solutions to problems.

Type III
Also practically orientated, likes problem-solving and may well prefer technical work to that involving social interaction.

Type IV
An abstract thinker with strong logical thought processes but not so comfortable with people and practical issues.

One of the most widely applied models of learning styles was devised by Honey and Mumford (1986). Their eighty item diagnostic questionnaire helps people to discover their own preferred learning style from among four key types (not dissimilar to those identified by Kolb):

Activist learner
Constantly seeks new experiences, opportunities and problems; likely to be good in role play and business games.

Reflective learner
Tends to think things through before acting.

Theorist learner
Likes to look for links and associations between ideas, events and situations and will tend to question everything.

Pragmatist learner
Prefers to see links between theory and practice.

That categorization of people is possible through the use of IQ tests (and aptitude tests) is undoubtedly true, and proponents of the tests strongly defend their use and value. However, many would argue that there is more to a person's capabilities than the 'g' factor of intelligence.

This quotient or measure of intelligence (which is thought to be a core ability facilitating individual powers of analysis and deductive reasoning) has been given the simple label 'g' (for general intelligence). However, its apparent simplicity arouses enormous controversy and passion particularly in the US where some have looked for (and found) correlations between IQ and socio-racial groups — and, from this, others have exploited information on what they perceive as correlations between IQ and social grouping, income grouping, class, and race to stir up division and strife.

In short, the IQ system may well be nearing the end of its useful life and is widely viewed as having only limited value.

(2)   Multiple Intelligence (MI)

One promising pretender to the pre-eminence enjoyed for a long time by the IQ system is multiple intelligence theory. Its originator, Howard Gardner (1999) conceptualizes intelligence as:

> *'. . . a bio-psychological potential to process information that can be activated in a cultural setting to solve problems or create products that are of value in a culture.'*

His analyses of many experimental (human) subjects, particularly of those with brain damage due to strokes, gave Gardner acute insights into the nature of human capabilities and intelligence. He startled the scientific world by adding an 's' to the word intelligence and, in his earlier work (1983), defined seven intelligences that he believes better reflect human capabilities than IQ alone. These he states as:

Verbal/linguistic intelligence. The ability to use language to effect; sensitivity in the use of words. Much of Western education with its emphasis on book learning is based on linguistic intelligence.

Logical-mathematical intelligence. Characterized by abstract reasoning and deduction capabilities, and problem solving. It is typical of 'scientific thinking', which tends to look for the recognition of abstract patterns.

Visual/spatial intelligence. 'Sight related' intelligence dependent on the ability to create and manipulate mental images.

Musical/rhythmic intelligence. The ability to recognize and manipulate sounds, tonal patterns, rhythms and melody are chief parts of this intelligence.

Bodily-kinaesthetic intelligence. Both fine and gross motor control of the body are part of this intelligence which is, overall, characterized by well-developed body language and the ability to manipulate objects.

Interpersonal intelligence. The ability to read other people's moods through their body language and other signs is characteristic of this intelligence. Its importance to management cannot be overstated!

Intra-personal intelligence. Self-awareness, introspection and self-reflection are necessary part of effective thinking. Intra-personal intelligence allows one to create an accurate self-model by which one can function in everyday life.

In his more recent work, Gardner (1999) identifies two further intelligences:

Naturalistic intelligence. Defined as the ability to relate to and understand the world of nature.

Spiritual intelligence. The capacity for spiritual and/or religious feelings found in many people.

Gardner also tentatively puts forward cases for Existential and Moral Intelligences but fails to convince even himself!

Everyone possesses ALL of the multiple intelligences, but the blend and balance in which they are present determine the overall characteristics of the individual. If, for instance, one of the intelligences is enormously in preponderance (at the expense of the others) then this will have a profound effect on personality and behaviour.

ACTION **ACTIVITY 4**

The following table summarizes the personal characteristics associated with Gardner's original seven intelligences. In the blank column, note down what you imagine would be the value of these characteristics in a learning organization.

MI	Personal characteristics	Value to LO
Interpersonal Intelligence	Sensitive to others and their views. Relates well to others and has lots of friends. Learns well through group work.	
Intra-personal Intelligence	Has good self-knowledge and uses this to operate effectively in life/work. Is reflective, perhaps introspective. Aware of what drives and motivates self—perhaps self-sufficient. Learns alone with individual projects.	
Verbal/ Linguistic Intelligence	Enjoys the use and power of language and good conversation. Enjoys reading/ writing. Enjoys 'play on words'. Learns by hearing/saying.	
Logical/ Mathematical Intelligence	Good with numbers/maths/ algebra/science and abstract patterns. Good spatial abilities. Learns by categorizing and classifying/looks for abstract patterns and relationships.	
Visual/ Spatial Intelligence	Discerning of patterns and colours. May have drawing & design skills. Good map/plan reader. Understands plans easily. Learns by visualization and imagery.	
Body/ Kinaesthetic Intelligence	Good mind–body connectivity/ physical control/spatial abilities. Enjoys physical activities, sports, etc. Learns through movement and use of bodily sensations.	

MI	Personal characteristics	Value to LO
Musical/ Rhythmic Intelligence	Musical — able to sing and whistle in tune. Rhythmical/ responsive to music. Enjoys music and perhaps music making. Learns through rhythm/music/melody.	

Compare your responses with our commentary in Appendix 1.

(3) Emotional Intelligence (EI)

Why do we get on well with some people and distrust others? Why do the brightest people seldom end up the richest? Why, given the same circumstances, do some people remain 'on top of things' whilst others sink into despair? What human qualities determine success? Clearly not IQ alone!

Emotional Intelligence and its linked Emotional Quotient (EQ) relate directly to the 'soft skills' that are nowadays greatly prized by many organizations. Dismissed by some as 'psycho-babble' (perhaps those who need it most!), high EI is now generally recognized as an essential component in the make-up of a good manager and effective team worker. Emotional Intelligence sprang from ideas on 'social intelligence', feelings, moods and emotions, first formalized in 1990 by Mayer, DiPaolo and Salovey in an article in the *Journal of Personality Assessment*. They looked at people's abilities to discern and identify the emotions represented by faces, abstract designs and colours. From their studies they concluded that there is a single competence for this ability to recognize emotional content — and that it is present in different people at different levels.

A further article in the same year by Salovey and Mayer, entitled *Emotional Intelligence*, brought together research from different areas and set out a widely accepted model for emotional intelligence. These two have progressively established a firmer basis for their theories and developed objective tests able to quantify people's emotional intelligence. In 1997 they defined EI as:

'. . . the ability to perceive emotions, to access and generate emotions so as to assist thought, to understand emotions and emotional knowledge, and to reflectively regulate emotions so as to promote emotional and intellectual growth.'

As Mayer explained in a 1999 interview (*Psychology Today*, vol. **32** issue 4 p. 20) when asked to explain the link between intellect and emotions:

> *'There are two sides to it. One side involves the intellect understanding emotion. The other side involves intellect reaching into the intellectual system and bringing about creative thoughts and ideas. The second side is hardest to pin down in the lab. But we believe it exists.'*

04-2

He further explained that the popular view of EI differs from the research findings and is often presented as little more than a list of traits such as optimism, persistence and warmth. He is worried that people involved with EI are simply encouraged to be as cheerful, energetic and happy as possible at work. Emotional Intelligence, believe its originators, has no right to dictate how anyone should feel at work.

Original EI theory: four branches	Developing EI theory: five categories
☛ Identifying Emotions ☛ Using Emotions ☛ Understanding Emotions ☛ Managing Emotions	☛ *Self-awareness*: observing yourself and recognising a feeling as it happens. ☛ *Managing emotions*: handling feelings so that they are appropriate; realizing what is behind a feeling; finding ways to handle fears and anxieties, anger, and sadness. ☛ *Motivating oneself*: channelling emotions in the service of a goal; emotional self-control; delaying gratification and stifling impulses. ☛ *Empathy*: sensitivity to others' feelings and concerns and taking their perspective; appreciating the differences in how people feel about things. ☛ *Handling relationships*: managing emotions in others; social competence and social skills.

The work of Mayer, Salovey and others has attracted considerable publicity and is heavily cited by Goleman in his books (*Emotional Intelligence*, 1995 and *Working With Emotional Intelligence*, 1998). Those with an eye for scientific purity have criticized areas of Goleman's books for some lack of objectivity but he, more than anyone, has brought the concepts of EI to public attention and has popularized the subject.

Goleman defines EI as:

> *'. . . referring to the capacity for recognizing our own feelings and those of others, for motivating ourselves, and for managing emotions well in ourselves and in our relationships.'*

ACTIVITY 5

On the basis of these various definitions, consider the following common attributes that are frequently ascribed to managers and decide which belong to the manager with a high EQ and which are more likely to belong to the manager with a lower EQ. To add a little zest to this exercise, think of people you know (even yourself) and decide which of the attributes best describe the chosen individual(s).

Words	High EQ Manager/Team Member	Low EQ Manager/Team Member
macho		
large ego		
empathic		
good-listener		
unsympathetic		
always right		
pass-the-buck		
understanding		
trustworthy		
untrustworthy		
adaptable		
inflexible		
honest		
dishonest		
aware		
unaware		
self-controlled		
uncontrolled		
optimistic		
pessimistic		
persuasive		
bullying		
caring		
team-player		
loner		
humorous		
cruel		
unpleasant		
pleasant		
self-centred		
uncaring		
motivating		
de-motivating		
charismatic		
boorish		
fault-finding		
complimentary		
communicative		
uncommunicative		

Attributes that describe your chosen individual(s):

Now read on.

In Goleman's Emotional Competence framework he recognizes two types of competence, namely personal competence and social competence. Personal competence determines how we manage ourselves and within this area Goleman recognizes three sub-competences, namely:

- ☛ Self-awareness
- ☛ Self-regulation
- ☛ Motivation.

All three concern self-knowledge and are dependent not only on introspection but also the ability to exercise self-control.

Social competence determines how we handle relationships. There are two parts to social competence:

- ☛ Empathy (awareness of others' feelings, needs and concerns)
- ☛ Social skills (adeptness at inducing desirable responses in others).

Under the heading of *empathy*, Goleman lists a number of very important management skills which include the ability to understand other people's feelings and perspectives, supporting people, providing customer service, delegation and sensitivity to group or political situations.

Perhaps even more important are the *social skills*. Within this area Goleman places listening skills, skills in presenting information, influence and conflict management, relationship building, team-work and leadership.

The Learning Organization

These competences, in accordance with the theme of his 1998 book are oriented towards work, teams and management. Indeed, most managers and executives would be very pleased to see these attributes exhibited by those in their organizations. But how many people can recognize EI in themselves or their colleagues? Although there remains much controversy over the accuracy and validity of testing for EI/EQ (redolent of the problems with IQ testing) there is a variety of tests now available. The best ones are multi-factorial and Mayer and Salovey have trade marked the term Multi Factor Intelligence Scale (MEIS). They believe that these tests will become an invaluable tool in the screening of candidates for selection and as an indicator for performance evaluation. 'Fun' tests can be taken on line at:

http://www.utne.com/azEQ.tmpl

and

http://www.queendom.com/cgi-bin/tests

Our emotions are thought to be associated with neurological structures in our lower, more primitive brain. EI theorists suggest that, although there is a basic genetic determination for EI, we have the capacity to modify our EI as we grow, age and learn. In contrast, IQ is thought to be a function of the upper, cerebral part of the brain and to have a higher level of genetic determinance, with relatively little capacity for change. So far, no link has been established between the two measures of intelligence.

(4) Neuro-Linguistic Programming (NLP)

If we accept the premise of EI that individual capabilities can be learned and behaviours can be modified, the concept of Neuro-Linguistic Programming (NLP) might be a useful tool in this respect. NLP targets and utilizes our EI competences in order to:

'Help people to become more competent at what they do and more in control of their thoughts, feelings and actions, more positive in their approach to life and better able to achieve results.'
(Harris 1999)

46

Richard Bandler (with a background in mathematics and psychology) and John Grinder (linguistics), working at the University of Santa Cruz, California in the 1970s, investigated how the most effective people achieve their results — they wanted to know how these people are able to influence others. They found that their 'successful' research subjects exhibited very similar and specific basic patterns of behaviour and thinking. Essentially these people were very effective communicators. This prompted the researchers to try to define the programmes or patterns of behaviour exhibited by these effective, successful people.

What they also professed to find was that other people could be trained or programmed to emulate or replicate these patterns of successful behaviour (or any other behaviour!) and to overlay them on their own behaviours and thereby increase their individual effectiveness.

The processes by which this behaviour modification or transformation is brought about is Neuro-Linguistic Programming — so called because the methods are heavily reliant on knowledge of brain structures and functions (neurology) and the use of linguistics to re-programme behaviours. Indeed, such is the perceived value and power of NLP techniques at present that a minor industry of practitioners and trainers has sprung up around it (and the term 'NLP' has been trademarked by Bandler).

Bandler (1979) defines NLP as:

> *'The study of the structure of subjective experience and what can be calculated from it.'*

As part of the 'NLP procedures' the brain functions and thought processes of individuals are studied. In this respect, NLP shares some of its techniques with those of hypnotism in which, of course, the successful hypnotist 'reads' subjects and is, by the use of special language and behaviour (a type of applied linguistics), able to modify a subject's behaviour. In brief, a very special type of communication is used.

NLP 'tools' have been systematized and include:

☞ *Sensory acuity and physiology* — that a person's thought processes influence physiology is obvious when, for example, a pleasurable experience, or embarrassing experience, or annoying experience is contemplated. Therefore, to 'read' the listener's 'state' by information gathering techniques is of advantage to the speaker — this includes reading clues in eye movements, breathing patterns and even minute clues such as pupil diameter and slight skin flushing.

☞ *The 'Meta-Model'* — this technique allows a practitioner to 'dig beneath the surface' — to find what in NLP is described as 'deep structure' underneath the 'surface structure'.

☞ *Representational systems* — because people think and represent knowledge in different ways (for example, auditory, visual and kinaesthetic thinkers), they may well have problems in communicating effectively with each other.

☞ *The 'Milton Model'* — named after the famous psychiatrist and hypnotherapist, Milton Erikson, it describes various linguistic patterns used by him to induce trance in his patients.

☞ *Eye Accessing Cues* — some clues to the subject's state can be 'read' by the practitioner from eye movements.

☞ *Submodalities* — one's perception/thoughts on one topic are 'coloured' by others. In NLP-speak, the structure affects the perception of content.

☞ *Metaprograms* — NLP is able to analyse, and harness, a person's outlooks and attitudes, for example a subtle distinction is drawn between people who are motivated toward goals and others who are motivated away from non-goals — analysis of the 'type' gives insights that can be used in that individual's programming.

For more information and lots of links look at:

http://www.nlp.com

NLP is now widely used in many fields including education, training, creativity, sales, counselling and psychotherapy. Many report considerable value from NLP in management training, particularly training for leadership attitudes and skills. NLP, it is claimed, has great potential for mental enrichment and enables people to see the world in a different way, to see a bigger picture — and from this to be able to see a greater number of possibilities and options than the person with a more limited perspective.

04-2-3 Collective Learning

Sadly for organizations, proven thinking about the factors which influence collective learning lags some way behind individual learning theory. The key question, which remains to be answered in a convincing and comprehensive manner, is how can groups of people learn effectively?

Technology is thought to be a great enabler in this field, and two parallel theories have emerged about how computers can facilitate group development:

- ☛ CSCW — Computer Supported Collaborative Working
- ☛ CSCL — Computer Supported Collaborative Learning.

Although there is a clear semantic distinction between the two, for the purposes of the learning organization, CSCW and CSCL are all but interchangeable: both concern the use of computer systems to share information and experience, to extend collective knowledge and to tackle problems collaboratively. The three main types of system suitable for collaborative working and learning are:

- ☛ *Communications systems* (synchronous text, audio, audio-graphics, and video communication; asynchronous electronic mail, computer conferencing, voicemail and fax)

- ☛ *Resource sharing systems* (synchronous screen-sharing and electronic whiteboards, concept mapping tools; asynchronous access to file systems and databases)

- ☛ *Group support systems* (project management systems, shared calendars, co-authoring tools, voting tools, ideas generation and brainstorming tools).

CASE STUDY: VIRTUAL TEAM WORKING

A regional training organization in the UK used a virtual team working system to manage a complex web design project. On its initial introduction by the project leader, there was some scepticism from team members (who represented a design company, a multimedia business, and various learning and management consultancies).

Over time, the improvement in project efficiency, communication and performance against targets became gradually apparent. When the project leader ran a review of satisfaction with the virtual system, the team's feedback was largely positive with particular praise for:

☞ The way the system's threaded discussion area effectively formed a virtual history of the project (highlighting critical events, problems and solutions).

☞ The contribution to collective understanding made by the system's editing facility. This enabled authorized users to edit designs and content, and display their modifications for comment by others.

☞ The way the system facilitated democratic decision making: prevailing views were apparent from users' contributions to discussions and comments on developing content; and the voting system had established clear preferences on critical design issues.

In their current state of development, collaborative systems do have some significant limitations militating against their utility for collective learning. Some basic problems are that:

☞ IT skills within most groups will probably vary considerably. The most IT-literate will, for example, feel more comfortable about experimenting with new tools and functions, and will get a lot more out of computer-supported collaborative exercises than the IT-terrified.

☞ Discussion-based IT systems can suffer from two types of ambiguity. First is the familiar ambiguity of words or phrases which can have more than one meaning. The second ambiguity is silence which can convey disagreement, lack of involvement or inability to participate.

☞ Knowledge storage and retrieval systems, usually databases, are only as effective as the input (and out-take) from group members. If only a few members of the group are using the system to find and post information, can the system really be said to be stimulating collective learning? All too often, the answer to that question will depend on the influence of those using the system to its fullest extent.

But the point raised in the earlier case study about the cumulative recording of project histories is an instructive one. The learning history (not necessarily IT-based) is one tool offered by some management thinkers as a way of stimulating, directing and evaluating collective learning in organizations. There are variations on the way the tool is designed and used, but typically the learning history is a paper document containing a narrative description of the organization's recent past. It describes critical events, changes, new initiatives and developments, significant performance, and so on.

To ensure as representative as possible a version of organizational history, those (or representatives of those) involved in the events contribute to chronicling the narrative, which tends to be confined to one of two columns. The other column is reserved for a commentary supplied by 'learning historians' — usually people from outside the organization with appropriate expertise.

Once the history has been compiled and the commentary completed, the document is reviewed within teams and is intended to feed into strategies for development at organizational, team and individual levels.

04-2

Still a relatively young technique, there is not a great deal of evidence at present about how successful the learning history is in bringing about collective learning. But one of its originators (George Roth of the Massachusetts Institute of Technology) has, through his work with various US companies such as Electro Components, identified certain conditions which are important for the learning history approach to succeed:

☞ Everyone in the organization should have the opportunity to contribute to its development (even if this is at one remove — i.e. by suggesting ideas to a representative from their part of the organization).

☞ When the learning history is reviewed, readers should 'take on the mindset of a beginner'. In effect this means reading with an open mind and suspending judgement.

☞ Whoever contributes to the learning history should be able to do so uncensored.

☞ There should be no fear of recrimination as a result of the process — amnesty should be offered to those harbouring guilty secrets!

and then I pushed the old MD under the tram!

The learning history technique borrows from the idea of oral tradition, where stories and proverbs, often articulating accumulated wisdom, are passed from generation to generation within discrete groups. Most of us understand that collective learning is possible at the level of ethnic grouping and even on a national basis: both are probably incremental processes which can however be speeded up by significant events or disasters. It would be instructive to compare the learning impact of World War II on those nations involved — superficially at least it appears that while the US, Germany and Japan all learned quickly and profitably from it, other states such as the UK and Russia did not.

Before closing this section, two more facets of collective learning should be mentioned — both of which have relevance for organizations. The first is the phenomenon of collective learning by regional clusters of organizations. Much research has been published recently about the impact of collective learning on the development of leading European regional clusters, predominantly made up of high technology SMEs. UK research published by Dr D Keeble and others (1998) has focused on Oxford and Cambridge and highlighted the following main findings:

☞ One of the principal means of knowledge sharing between regional businesses happens via labour market movement. In short, people who develop expertise in one organization take it to another when they change jobs. If they remain on good terms with their former employer, partnerships may occur.

☞ Coupled with this is a factor which may be peculiar to the prestige university towns of Oxford and Cambridge. Personal networks linking regional businesses appear to be far stronger than would usually be expected. People in similar positions were often contemporaries at school, university or both: they therefore have a similar background and outlook.

☞ Local supply chains are also key to the dissemination of learning. The communication tends to be vertical, but not necessarily one-way.

☞ Local service providers, particularly in the areas of research, consultancy, education and training, also contribute to regional cross-pollination. Even where their direct or immediate impact is not great, their role in facilitating networks contributes significantly to the exchange of ideas.

☞ Local government and non-government agencies can have a similar impact in facilitating research, growth and networking.

One apparent lesson from the research into regional clusters is that market forces have a quicker and perhaps greater impact on learning transfer than interventionist policies. However, the final facet of collective learning we will discuss is pure intervention and operates at a global level.

CASE STUDY:
SUSTAINABLE DEVELOPMENT
NETWORKS

04-2

In 1992 the United Nations established a series of Sustainable Development Networks. Their objective was to enable developing countries to learn (primarily from each other) about policies and practices related to sustainable development. The global network now links together government and private sector organizations, universities, non-governmental organizations and individuals in over 90 countries spread over Asia, Africa and Latin America. Information Communications Technology provides the linking framework.

The broad benefits of Sustainable Development Networks have been identified as increased efficiency in the use of development resources, less duplication of activities, reduced communication costs and global access to information and human resources.

The Sustainable Development Networking Programme in India is a one-stop access point for information and resources on an enormous range of issues from agriculture to health, to climatic changes and Third World debt. Its founders envisaged it as:

- A centralized, exhaustive electronic repository of information on issues, events, government policies, and organizations related to sustainable development
- An active mechanism for communication, coordination and networking among NGOs, community groups, business enterprises, academic and research institutions, and government bodies on issues relating to sustainable development.
- A proactive, value-driven force monitoring policies and events, and facilitating partner organizations and collaborative networks in pursuit of policy changes to create a conducive environment for sustainable development.

The website for SDNP-India can be visited at:

http://sdnhq.undp.org/mirrors/as/india/

04-3 THE STRATEGIC IMPACT OF LEARNING

04-3 THE STRATEGIC IMPACT OF LEARNING

04-3-1 The Impact of Learning on Organizational Performance

The premise on which the learning organization concept is often 'sold' is that it will improve organizational, and more specifically business, performance. But whose word do we have for this? Obviously we have the word of Peter Senge and his associates, and we have the word of many other management thinkers and consultants who have got in on what Senge (2000) himself has described as 'a fad'. These people clearly have a vested interest!

The first bottle to the stranger at the back!

Little empirical evidence has been published to support the contention that learning organizations are successful organizations. Honourable mentions should go to Pettigrew and Whipp (1991) who published a study covering four UK industries, showing that those with effective learning processes at all level of organization tended to be more successful than the rest. And there is, it has to be said, a considerable number of case studies describing how companies — usually blue chip — are or became learning organizations.

www.universal-manager.co.uk

PAUSE TO REFLECT

What organizations can you think of which might deserve the accolade of learning organization?

Now read on.

Some of the most commonly touted names in this context are Skandia (the Swedish insurance company), Ericsson, Nokia, Amoco, EDS, Chrysler, Amazon, Toyota, and Matsushita — the US and Japanese predominance might be expected, but the strong showing of Scandinavian countries is interesting and may be indicative of cultural predisposition to learning (or at least not to obstruct collective learning).

04-3

CASE STUDY:
THE 'STUMBLING STONE' PROJECT

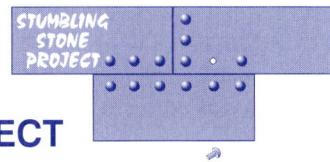

This was a quality-driven project which took place at Odense Steel shipyard. The main goal agreed by management and the consultants (KIO) was to involve yard workers in an effective and sustainable way in quality improvement.

A pragmatic approach was taken in which individuals and teams were encouraged to identify hindrances or constraints to their work ('stumbling stones') — and the work-force was empowered to find ways to remove these constraints. Success was indicated when those who had first identified stumbling stones reported that they were no longer encountering the same problems. The many small improvements and removal of hindrances brought about by the project's approach were directly responsible for productivity increases and efficiencies.

Learning was reinforced and knowledge exchanged in 'innovation teams' of three to five team members per 50 – 100 employees. In this way, through continuous improvement and learning at individual and team levels, better ways of working were developed and disseminated within the yard.

Summarized from the presentation of Ole Hinz (KIO) to the ECLO conference, 1997.

The Learning Organization

It might be argued that improvements in productivity or profitability do not strictly constitute evidence of strategic impact. To have true strategic impact, learning should be seen to influence organizational strategy in some way.

☞ *Learning as a strategy*. It is not uncommon to read mission or value statements professing a profound organizational commitment to learning or to the development of people. Yet how many organizations can back up such a claim with a track record of long-term, consistent and coherent investment in learning? Outstanding examples of this kind of commitment tend to be confined to industries where R & D has historical strength: the pharmaceuticals and high technology industries for instance. In these sectors, it is customary to devote large budgets and teams to exploratory projects with planned durations of three, five and ten years — and all of this in the knowledge that such projects might deliver nothing of value.

Where R & D does not have such a strong link to competitive edge, particularly in the service and public sectors, true commitment to learning tends to be on a smaller scale. Although most UK government departments and agencies spend well above the national average on training and development, it is doubtful whether any could make a convincing case for the existence of a long term strategy of improved performance through learning. In the service sector, there are often widespread strategic initiatives with some link to organizational learning: the almost blanket introduction of loyalty schemes during the 1990s was a case in point. Yet, the proportion of retail organizations which have genuinely used their loyalty schemes to learn about customers is probably minimal.

☞ *Learned strategy*. Henry Mintzberg (1994) notes a divergence in many organizations between intended and realized strategy.

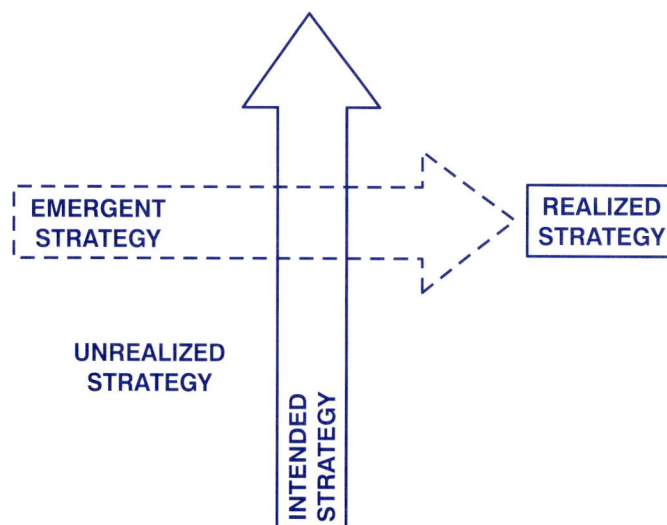

The previous illustration makes the point that it is quite possible (and perhaps common) to reach or surpass planned targets by means other than those intended. Learned strategy is one of the ways organizations diverge from their planned paths, often when something valuable is learned unintentionally (perhaps at the periphery of the organization) which later becomes central to corporate plans. One of the best known examples from recent times occurred when research scientists at Pfizer chanced upon the formula for Viagra while engaged in cardiovascular research. The drug that emerged accidentally from their experiments transformed not only the research and marketing strategy of Pfizer, but global markets for non-medicinal drugs.

04-3

ACTIVITY 6

How great is the influence of learning on your own organization's strategy?

(a) When strategy is formulated, how is collective learning taken into account?

(b) In strategic and business planning processes, how far down and across the organizations are views and ideas sought?

(c) How feasible is it that an unplanned development (like the discovery of Viagra) could shape your organization's strategy? Would the organization be flexible enough to adapt to such a development within less than a year?

Now read on.

04-3-2 Demonstrating the Impact of Organizational Learning and Development

The business case for the learning organization, or, put another way, the organizational imperative for investing in learning, must be something of a leap of faith. How does one measure the cost return on a change in cultural outlook? What is the return on investment (ROI)? The acronym ROI can also mean Return on Information — a related measure in this context is Return on Intellectual Capital (RIC).

A suitable but somewhat subjective view can be gained by the careful employment of well-designed 'before and after' attitudinal surveys of personnel, suppliers and customers/clients. More objective measures can be gleaned from monitoring data covering key indicators such as the bottom line, absenteeism and staff turnover. These all help to give a good measure of the success of any innovation aimed at quality improvement.

One UK initiative, which has provided many organizations with an added incentive to evaluate the impact of their learning, is Investors in People (IIP). IIP is a quality standard centred on systems and practices of people development and performance management. In order to be recognized as an Investor in People, an organization needs to be successfully measured against twelve performance indicators. Among the requirements specified by those indicators are:

- A strong and demonstrable commitment to people development
- Clear aims and objectives which are understood by all employees
- Learning and development activities that are linked to organizational aims and objectives
- Line managers who are active and effective in supporting learning and development.

For a full breakdown of the IIP standard, visit the Awarding Body's website at http://iipuk.co.uk

The particular relevance of IIP here is that the standard requires organizations to demonstrate and communicate the impact of their investment in learning at three levels: organizational, team (departmental or unit level) and individual. Overwhelmingly, this is the part of the standard that organizations struggle with.

A breakdown of some of the problems commonly encountered can give us some strong clues about generic difficulties with measuring learning's impact:

- *Breakdown in transfer.* There is a common failure to spell out clearly what planned learning is intended to achieve. At the same time, it is rare to find learning designed with the recipient's work role and context in mind. As a result, employee learning is seldom applied in full. Because the new behaviour expected as a result of training is not defined, it doesn't materialize.

- *Isolation.* Even where the purpose and expected outcomes of learning are clearly defined, it is rare for this definition to extend beyond individual behaviour. Yet learning and development is financed by employers on the understanding that it will help improve organizational performance. This means organizations should plan and prioritize corporate development needs (linked to corporate objectives), while team and individual learning needs should be guided by corporate needs. And crucially, line managers and employees must understand how the individual development fits into the wider corporate plan.

- *Quantity not quality.* The initial reaction in most organizations attempting to strengthen processes for the evaluation of learning is to devise numerical measures: numbers of training hours or days; numbers of trainees; training and development costs; ratios of expenditure to beneficiaries; downtime, etc.

> We're behind target on training days this quarter. Perkins, I want you to attend 14 courses by next Friday!

Quantitative, and particularly financial, measures *are* important, but they rarely tell us how effective learning has been. Qualitative measures are far more helpful in this respect. Although they are rarely easy to create, they should get to the heart of why the training was required in the first place — therefore effective learning measures are inextricable from effective learning objectives.

The Learning Organization

What then are the solutions to these common problems with learning evaluation? Most methods practised today were devised to address the impact of training and development rather than learning in its full sense. Nevertheless, two of the more successful approaches (described below) are easily adaptable to cover any planned learning activity which takes place over a finite period of time.

(1) The Kirkpatrick Model

The Kirkpatrick model, developed in 1959 by a former professor at the University of Wisconsin, is based on a four-level approach:

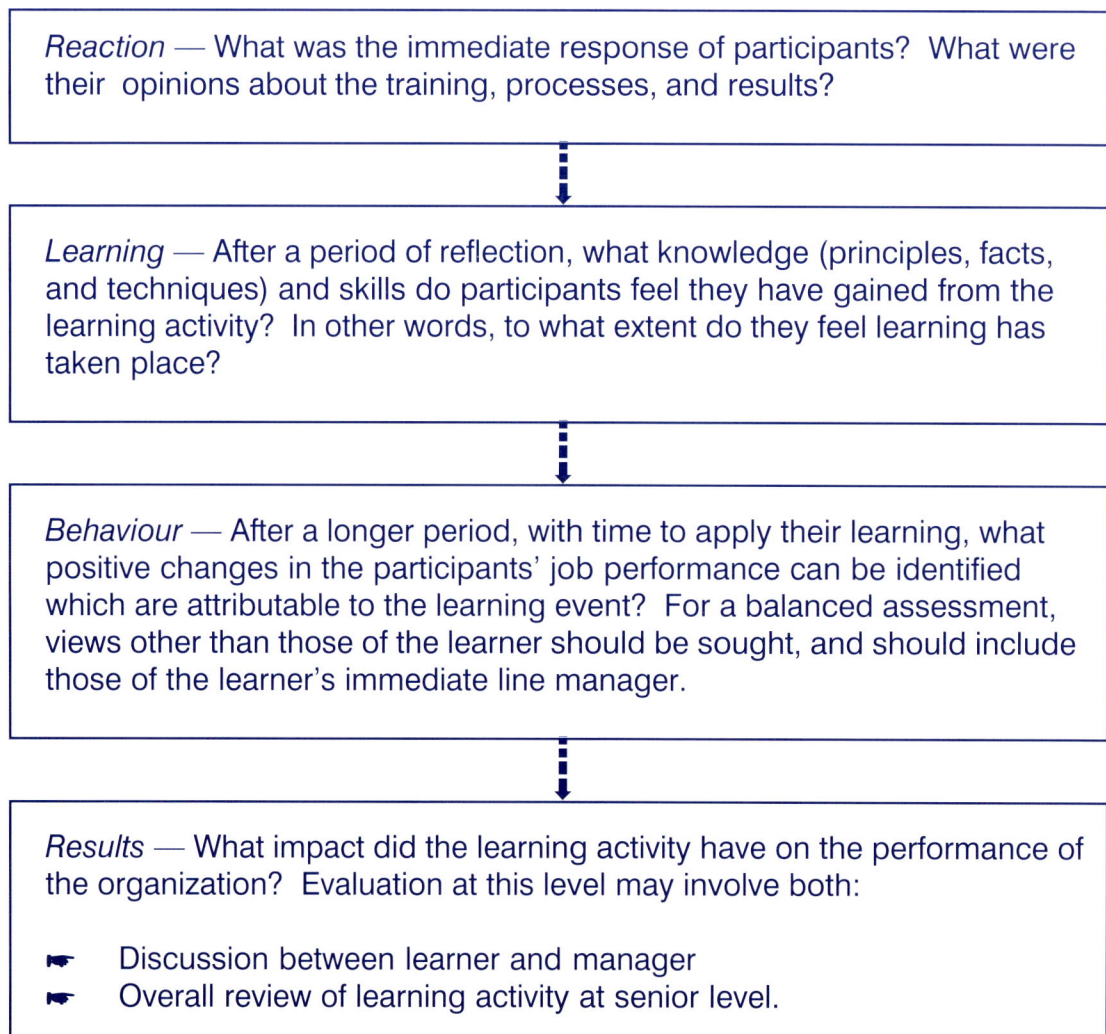

> *Reaction* — What was the immediate response of participants? What were their opinions about the training, processes, and results?

> *Learning* — After a period of reflection, what knowledge (principles, facts, and techniques) and skills do participants feel they have gained from the learning activity? In other words, to what extent do they feel learning has taken place?

> *Behaviour* — After a longer period, with time to apply their learning, what positive changes in the participants' job performance can be identified which are attributable to the learning event? For a balanced assessment, views other than those of the learner should be sought, and should include those of the learner's immediate line manager.

> *Results* — What impact did the learning activity have on the performance of the organization? Evaluation at this level may involve both:
>
> ☛ Discussion between learner and manager
> ☛ Overall review of learning activity at senior level.

(2) Results Oriented HRD Model

This model (illustrated on the following page) takes into account the total human resource development process, from needs analysis to communicating results. Although complex in its full form, this 18-step model is adaptable to a variety of learning contexts.

www.universal-manager.co.uk

(1) Carry out needs analysis and develop learning objectives.

(2) Identify the purpose of evaluation. (For example, evaluation will identify the contribution of the learning activity to improved individual performance.)

(3) Establish baseline data. (For example, if learning is intended to improve standards of customer service, one appropriate baseline measure might be the number of complaints received.)

(4) Select evaluation method (i.e. what data will be collected and how).

(5) Determine evaluation strategy — who will conduct the evaluation, where and when.

(6) Finalize learning objectives — some adjustment may be necessary in view of the defined evaluation method and strategy.

04-3

(7) Estimate costs and benefits.

(8) Prepare and present a proposal (assuming that authorization is required for expenditure).

(9) Design evaluation tools, e.g. questionnaires, tests, attitude surveys, interviews.

(10) Define and develop learning content — even if an off-the-shelf learning solution such as an existing course or pack is to be purchased, some customization is usually advisable for employee learning.

(11) Design or select instruction methods — don't forget that some learning occurs via self-study.

(12) Test and adjust learning solutions — a luxury not available to many small firms.

(13) Implement learning activity.

(14) Collect data as planned.

(15) Analyse and interpret data.

(16) Adjust learning delivery — if it has not produced the desired results.

(17) Calculate Return on Investment (ROI) — in simple terms learning ROI is calculable by the formula:

$$\text{Return} = \frac{\text{net learning benefits (or savings)}}{\text{learning costs (or investment)}}$$

(18) Communicate results — to HR staff or external providers so that delivery can be improved; to management for decision making purposes, and to participants to see how they performed.

04-3-3 What Does a Learning Organization Look Like?

So, how does an organization that claims to be a 'Learning Organization' differ from one that makes no such claim? It may well be that an organization is, in fact, behaving as a learning organization without really realizing that it can be categorized as one. Others, despite a proud and substantial commitment to learning, are far from achieving the ideal.

The following Activity is based on a model of the learning organization devised by David Towler (1998), Dean of Action Research and Continuing Management Development at Oxford Brookes University. Although one might quibble with its wording and coverage, Towler's model provides a comprehensive and rigorous standard.

Use each of the model's statements to assess the current processes and practices in your organization. Think about how far your organization measures up to the ideal presented and where there is room for improvement.

Maximum value will be derived from the exercise if you are able to arrange for it be completed by several people from your organization, and if time can be set aside for a discussion of responses.

ACTIVITY 7

(1)   *A Learning Organization makes a commitment from the top to create an environment of individual, team and organizational learning to achieve its business aims:*

(a)   The organization promotes learning by continually tracking its business environment (e.g. via organized competitive intelligence gathering).

(b)   The organization ensures all employees are aware of and fully involved in developing its vision and aims (or whichever key statements guide the behaviour, direction and aspiration of the organization's people).

(c) The organization ensures all employees at all levels work together to achieve individual and collective growth through learning.

(d) The organization ensures that individuals and teams are given every possible encouragement and support to grow and develop their level of responsibility, creativity and competence.

04-3

(2) *A Learning Organization promotes the exchange of information and joint learning between employees to create a more knowledgeable and effective workforce:*

(e) The organization establishes group working across traditional organizational boundaries on live business issues and problems as a major feature of its operation (e.g. through quality circles, task forces and project teams).

(f) The organization achieves self-managed learning by groups and individuals as normal practice throughout the whole of its workforce.

(g) The organization creates collective learning opportunities by bringing together individuals with a variety of skills, knowledge and technologies.

(3)   A Learning Organization takes action to create learning communities and to develop a culture of lifelong learning throughout its workforce:

(h)   The organization ensures that all employees are provided with incentives, resources and opportunities to continually develop their individual learning throughout their working lives.

(i)   The organization ensures all individuals develop themselves towards agreed goals (often within the scope of an appraisal or performance review process).

(j)   The organization creates opportunities for individuals to work collectively to reflect on, clarify and improve their understanding of their working environment in order to improve their capability to take decisions and action.

(k)   The organization builds a sense of commitment by encouraging groups to develop shared visions and values for the future development of the organization (related to point (b)).

(4)   A Learning Organization takes action to turn individual and group learning into organizational learning:

(l)   The organization evaluates its investment in learning to assess achievement and plan for future learning.

(m)   The organization evaluates the effect of learning on its culture, values, systems and performance.

(n)   The organization evaluates the effect of learning on its business strategy and its position in its business environment.

04-3

Now read on.

04-4 LEARNING NEEDS ANALYSIS

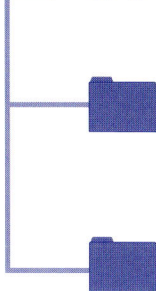

04-4

04-4 LEARNING NEEDS ANALYSIS

04-4-1 Analysing Learning Needs

Throughout this dossier we stress that learning and training are not the same — perhaps it would be more helpful to say that training is a means of learning, one of many subsets, for there is a great variety of ways that learning can take place.

ACTIVITY 8

List five learning methods you have experienced which did not involve attending a training course.

Compare your response with our suggestions in the commentary in Appendix 1.

The reason for stressing this distinction again is that clarity about the process expected to occur (learning) is essential in order to achieve an accurate identification of the need for that process (learning needs analysis). Systems thinking — Senge's fifth discipline — comes into play here.

CASE STUDY: ASSERTIVENESS TRAINING

'Put Your Foot Down'

ASSERTIVENESS TRAINING

Jane Harris — PA to John Butcher (Operations Director) — signed up for a course of assertiveness training. Along with other staff members in the organization, Jane felt she needed to become more confident at work, particularly when dealing with her line manager.

As line manager, John signed off the training application and Jane duly attended. Some weeks after the course, John asked her in passing how it had gone.

'It was quite good,' was Jane's opinion, 'The main thing I learned was that everyone at work has rights. You need to stand up for your own, but be aware of the rights of others at the same time.'

'Sounds like a load of baloney to me', replied her line manager. The assertiveness course wasn't mentioned again.

04-4

The point of that little vignette was to illustrate a problem besetting learning needs analysis in organizations of all kinds. Most learning needs analysis is single loop (identify a problem, find a solution: lacking confidence, do some assertiveness training). If the protagonists in our case study had engaged in double loop thinking, they would undoubtedly have concluded that the problem was with the line manager – employee working relationship. Training of some kind might have been appropriate, but whatever the solution, it should have involved *both* employee and line manager, preferably together, and it should have stimulated them to re-appraise the basis of the working relationship. A frank and equal one-to-one discussion might have satisfied all those requirements, but with a predisposition on both sides not to challenge the status quo, there was no way such a solution would have occurred.

An open mind is vital in learning needs analysis. Assumptions about, or ignorance of, available solutions inevitably narrow the field of enquiry and reduce the chances of identifying and addressing real needs. The tendency in many organizations is to identify *training* needs during appraisal or performance review sessions — the question posed is 'What sort of training is appropriate for this person?' The question should be: 'How does this person need to perform better?' For collective needs analysis of course this question will broaden to 'How does the organization or team need to improve performance?'

Whether the needs are individual or collective, the tried and trusted method among HR professionals is gap analysis: identifying where we are now, where we want to be, and what is the gap between the two positions.

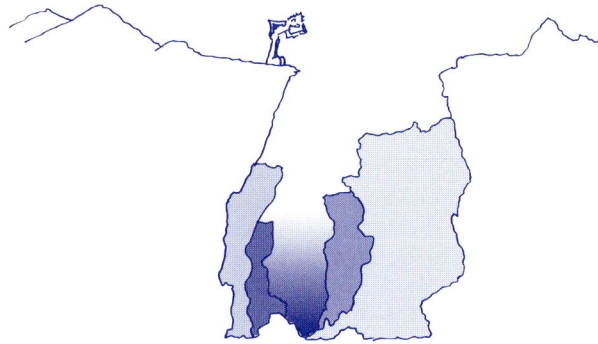

When using gap analysis to identify learning needs, both the start and destination points need to be expressed in terms of behaviour, otherwise the desired learning impact (changed behaviour) may be obscure. This is fine when working in charted territory, for instance towards a quality standard or within a competence framework — the endpoint is pre-defined and the start point can be located with reasonable objective certainty. It is much harder when there is no map — realistic destinations and accurate current positions become rather difficult to fix.

PAUSE TO REFLECT

Besides the 'off-the-shelf' standards provided by quality standards and competence frameworks, how does your organization go about identifying gaps or areas for development?

Now read on.

Some of the more common methods used to help with gap analysis are:

☞ *Benchmarking.* Using research and investigative methods to establish industry norms and best practices. One drawback with benchmarking is that sufficient detail on those competitive practices worth knowing about will be closely guarded. Another is that benchmarking can foster a 'just good enough' mentality — but successful organizations are not content to simply measure up to industry standards.

- *Historical performance analysis.* Identifying past trends in actual performance against targets. The problem here is that it is not safe to assume that areas showing the greatest divergence between planned and actual performance are indicative of the strongest development need. A great many factors not related to capability might account for the variation.

- *Internal review.* Whether by SWOT analysis or employee survey, this approach relies on collective opinion. Organized effectively, this democratic method may yield useful insights, but total reliance upon it risks insularity.

- *External review.* This might involve customer surveys; analysis of complaints; communication with suppliers, distributors and partners; or a Delphi study where expert panels are consulted about critical issues.

04-4

ACTION **ACTIVITY 9**

Use the table below to note down the practices adopted in your organization to identify learning needs. Note that we have continued the gap analysis approach: the assumption is therefore that different methods and/or sources will be used to specify:

- The current position
- The desired destination.

The gap to be bridged will be identified by comparing the two.

Level	Current position	Gap	Desired destination
Organization			
Team/ Department/ Unit			
Individual			

Compare your response with our suggestions in Appendix 1.

04-4-2 The Competency-based Approach

Competency or competence? There is a distinction between the two which is essentially transatlantic.

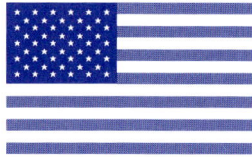

The US understanding of competencies sees them as a rich mix of personal characteristics: defining them can help predict how people will behave. Many organizations use competency profiling and testing as an aid to selection.

In the UK, competences concentrate on the job role rather than the person: they define the tasks that need to be performed, and (occasionally) the skills and knowledge required to perform tasks to the required standard.

The American concept of competencies was influenced most strongly by Richard Boyatzis (1982). Boyatzis saw competencies as a means of defining superior performers, particularly among management grades. He defined competencies as complex aptitudes made up of three elements: motive, self-image and skill. Boyatzis' ideas have been influential in the UK too, particularly in large organizations able to devote time and effort to competency definition. But the UK definition of competence has been most strongly shaped by the National Council for Vocational Qualifications (NCVQ) — now the Qualifications and Curriculum Authority (QCA). Here, a competence is more about the job than the person doing it, and competence definitions tend to focus on the outputs of the job, the range of situations in which the job must be carried out and, in some models, the knowledge and understanding the person requires.

Although this understanding of competence has been applied in the development of hundreds of National Vocational Qualifications, specifying performance standards across most industries and at all levels of organization, it appears to be less successful at management level than the more complex US model.

In practice, it appears that organizations adopting competency/competence frameworks tend to evolve a kind of hybrid approach mixing input and output specifications. Typically this will define the behaviour expected in key contexts (such as in project management or client-facing), and link this to the skills, knowledge and personality traits thought to result in the required behaviour.

Competence or competency definition has a clear utility for learning needs analysis. By constructing a competence framework an organization can specify:

☞ The performance expected of employees in key functions
☞ The skills and knowledge employees are expected to possess
☞ The range of situations in which they are expected to perform competently
☞ Internal progression routes in terms of competence development, promotion and financial reward.

The best examples of organizational competence frameworks are comprehensive (covering all levels of the organization), inclusive (relating to employees in all functions and of all types of employment status) and are integrated in key HRM processes such as recruitment and selection, appraisal, human resource planning and so on.

04-4

ACTIVITY 10

What are the primary competences required of managers in your organization?

Compare your response with our commentary in Appendix 1.

04-5 DEVELOPING A LEARNING CULTURE

04-5

04-5 DEVELOPING A LEARNING CULTURE

Most managers appreciate that the extent to which their people will learn and apply learning is greatly influenced by that amorphous collection of attitudes, perceptions, beliefs and habits often described as organizational culture. The difficulty comes with pinning down those aspects of organizational culture which promote or enrich learning, and those which inhibit or stifle it. Even more difficult is to set about changing organizational culture.

The organization's culture of working lunches
appeared to be undermining productivity

In this section, we define some of the key elements present in the culture of learning organizations, and look at strategies that can be employed to build such a culture. One enlightening and often amusing way to start off the exercise is to turn the issue on its head and pose the question: what could we do to sabotage learning in our organization?

ACTIVITY 11

Note down a few ways that your organization could effectively sabotage learning.

Now read on.

Rosabeth Moss Kanter (1983) in her book *The Change Masters* suggests five ways to stifle innovation, creativity and learning:

- Any idea from a subordinate must be regarded with suspicion. And why? Because it is new and because it is from below.
- To keep people on their toes, always express criticisms of them and their work freely. Never praise, and let them know they can be dismissed at any time.
- When problems occur treat them as a sign of failure of those involved — and make sure that they realize this.
- Treat openness as a sign of weakness and always make decisions to reorganize or to change policies in secret. Spring such changes onto people unexpectedly — this also helps to keep them on their toes.
- Above all, never forget that you and the management team are the most important people in the organization and that the executive already knows everything important that there is to know about management and business organization.

Goleman (1998) provides a number of strategies that he suggests are likely to lower performance and induce cynicism, exhaustion and burnout — to 'achieve' this, managers should:

04-5

- Ensure that work overload occurs (continually demanding greater output from fewer resources)
- Impose accountability without authority (lack of autonomy)
- Fail to give credit or praise (lack of reward)
- 'Divide and rule' (isolation from others in the organization)
- Promote inequality and unfairness (e.g. of executives' perks and pay)
- Value conflicts — create situations where there is a conflict between work and personal values (e.g. cutting corners in quality or health and safety for the sake of productivity).

This 'negative planning' approach can provide a great deal of cynical fun! But there is more to it than that. It provides warnings of practices the organization should avoid at all costs (some of which might currently be in evidence), and when we turn it around it should constitute a list of all those things an organization must get right if learning is to thrive. There is also a subtle learning point in the exercise: many of us find it easier to think of problems than solutions. Where negative planning or brainstorming gets a better response than traditional, right-way round exercises, this may be indicative of a pessimistic culture.

04-5-1   Key Elements in Learning Culture

Organizational culture can be defined in a number of ways, but there is broad agreement that it comprises three interdependent components:

BEHAVIOUR

CULTURE

VALUES   PRACTICES   NORMS

- *Values* encapsulate collective beliefs about the organization's *raison d'être*. They guide the ethical behaviour of the organization. If an organization's mission or vision is purely about returning a profit, then its cultural values will be restricted within the financial dimension. Many successful organizations have an altruistic element within their value systems; for instance IKEA retains its original commitment to helping to create 'a better everyday life for the majority of people'.

- *Norms* are shared expectations about the way the organization's employees should behave. In many cases of sexual harassment at work, the (unacceptable) defence of the perpetrators is that they were only behaving in accordance with tacitly accepted norms. Another example of normal behaviour in some organizations is seen in the 'long hours' culture which still claims many victims.

- *Practices* are a mix of formal and informal habits that apply in the workplace. Typical formal practices might be induction, team meetings and the annual Christmas 'do'. Informal extensions of these might include initiation rites, 'corridor conferences' and Friday afternoons in the pub.

As might be imagined, in most organizations the boundaries and reactions between these three elements are usually complex: practices can become norms, values should drive norms and practices, but when stated and true values are in conflict, the organization's normal behaviour and practices will tend to undermine the values it expresses to the world.

PAUSE TO REFLECT

What types of values, norms and practices might be associated with a learning organization?

Now read on.

Most contributors to the theory of the learning organization present a great many ideas about the kinds of cultural features that are to be found in such a unit. An analysis of points about which there is general agreement would probably find a consensus along the following lines:

☞ Part of the organization's intrinsic purpose should be continuous improvement to the benefit of its customers, its people and society as a whole. Learning should be valued as the driver of continuous improvement and renewal.

☞ Whether they are written, unwritten or a combination of both, the rules of behaviour should promote risk taking, experimentation and challenge. Openness and 'no blame' should be watch words.

☞ Formal and informal practices should enable frequent and frank review of performance, and constant exchange of information and ideas.

04-5

The recommendations put forward by Pedler and Aspinall (1998) are typical of the advice given on this subject:

☞ Discussions on policy and running the organization must not be confined to boardroom discussion but should go beyond the CE's office to the 'shopfloor' — executives and managers must listen to the workers! We might categorize this as a norm — the expected behaviour is participative.

☞ All in the organization, and particularly managers, must seek out tensions and barriers — close examination of these can lead to creative solutions. The underlying value is that the organization and its people should not be afraid of ambiguity, complexity or dissonance.

☞ Get away from the all too frequent 'winner–loser' scenario for resolving difficulties so that people can admit mistakes and all can learn from them. Again, we might consider this to be an example of a cultural value where mistakes are allowable in the pursuit of learning.

☞ Use IT-based Knowledge Management (KM) tools and methods to keep everyone in the organization well-informed — according to Pedler and Aspinall, widespread ICT practices will empower people to make decisions and take action.

☞ Ensure frequent internal dialogue between peers and departments, and external dialogue with customers and suppliers. This is a call for a mix of informal and formal communication practices.

These are five very commonly encountered suggestions about the way a learning organization behaves — it would certainly be possible to find another five hundred equally sensible recommendations, on similar themes. But for organizations trying to introduce and spread a learning culture, isolated suggestions like these (however practical they may be) are difficult to work with. How many organizations for example have introduced 'state of the art' ICT equipment in a bid to improve the internal flow of knowledge only to encounter passive resistance from the majority, and over-enthusiasm from a minority of employees?

Defining what a learning culture will look like is usually the easy part — changing attitudes and behaviour is much harder.

04-5-2   Building a Learning Culture

As with many other kinds of change or development programme, the experience of those who have tried to build learning organizations suggests that an effective way to proceed is by increments. Reported by Hodgson (1995), Theresa Barnett of TSB Staff College suggests that there is no need to tackle the whole organization at the same time. Efforts can be concentrated on small areas to create nuclei of good practice that will 'infect' others around them — indeed, given appropriate information transfer systems and suitable resources and encouragement, these learning nuclei will learn from one another as momentum gathers.

These nuclei may be construed as work teams, organizational tiers or work processes. One approach, loosely based on the Investors in People model, is to concentrate on breaking through in four areas:

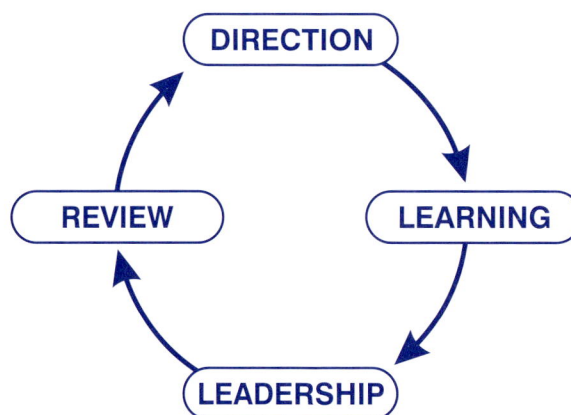

```
              DIRECTION
           ↗            ↘
    REVIEW                LEARNING
           ↖            ↙
              LEADERSHIP
```

(1) Direction

Starting with the top team, learning organizations must be effective at defining and communicating the direction they are headed. It doesn't matter whether the practice is to set goals, objectives or targets or to define entire behaviour rating systems, there needs to be a widespread, almost instinctive grasp of the organization's direction, and how this guides collective and individual endeavour.

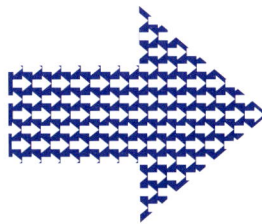

Some of the ways many successful firms instil this appreciation in their employees include ensuring wide participation in strategic and business planning; linking team and individual performance objectives to strategic objectives; and through constant reinforcement of key messages using all available communication formats.

04-5

(2) Leadership

In *The Fifth Discipline* Senge (1990) quotes William O'Brien, CE of the Hanover Insurance Group, as follows:

> *'Why don't people create such [learning] organizations? I think the answer is leadership. People have no real comprehension of the type of commitment it requires to build such an organization.'*

With reference to leadership styles, O'Brien points out that 'classic leadership' is about setting goals and making decisions. In such an organization, the leader figure assumes even greater importance when there is a crisis and the dangerous over-dependence of the organization on a single individual becomes apparent.

He goes on to say that, in contrast, leaders in a learning organization are teachers, designers and stewards employing a range of skills and styles — building shared visions (rather than imposing ideas from above), helping others to see their essential role in the organization (not just their own small part of it). Effective leaders have the courage to challenge the status quo, to examine their mental models and test organizational systems; and instil that courage in others.

The Learning Organization

It's important to be clear that the term 'leader' is not synonymous with 'manager' or 'director'. Leadership – in the forms of creativity, coaching, guidance, inspiration and motivation – might originate from any part of an organization. In a fast changing business environment, to immediate colleagues, the firm's resident expert in, say, SAP technology might be a stronger source of leadership than the Chief Executive. Many organizations have realized the importance of developing leadership at all levels:

☞ In some cases it may simply be about empowering front-line employees to make decisions, as seen in the hospitality chain which authorizes its people to spend up to £1,250 correcting customer service problems (reported in an ICS survey 'The Future of Customer Service' — 2000)

☞ It may extend to the creation of self-managed teams, an innovation recently piloted by the UK retailer Marks & Spencer with its Autograph collection

☞ With smaller firms or project teams, it is possible to have an 'adhocratic' arrangement where there is no hierarchy at all, and where the aim is to ensure that every team member has the competences, the resources and the confidence to take the lead when appropriate.

Instilling the confidence and independence required in non-hierarchical leaders is no easy task, particularly where the subjects are used to being led. Returning to the example of Marks & Spencer; after the retailer's dramatic restructuring over 1999 and 2000, one significant change was that the sales supervisor position was removed and cashiers were authorized to deal with till problems such as over-rings themselves. Yet for some time after the change had been implemented, most cashiers persisted in ringing the 'supervisor bell' when they had a difficulty . . . despite the fact that there was no longer a supervisor to respond.

This example is symptomatic of the 'denial' stage familiar to anyone who has ever been involved in implementing organizational change. Its particular relevance here is that leaders are not made overnight, and where organizations wish to devolve authority and responsibility, it is critical to provide the information, support and time needed for a successful transition.

84

ACTIVITY 12

What support strategies might your organization put in place if it wished to encourage multi-layered leadership?

Compare your ideas with our commentary in Appendix 1.

However, the reality in many organizations tends to the undemocratic; line managers tend to be the appointed and therefore expected source of leadership for subordinate employees. In such organizational structures, it is the line manager who provides the closest model of behaviour to subordinates; who is in day to day contact with them and best able to observe how they work; who — in short — has the greatest responsibility for maximizing individual performance. Many organizations and many managers, after the era of down-sizing and re-structuring, have been slow to appreciate the onus this places on the line manager to act as mentor and coach to employees. As a consequence, one of the greatest barriers to success in many organizations is the low level of competence in people management.

04-5

(3) Learning Development

The mistake commonly made once the edict has been issued ('We shall strive to become a learning organization') is to assume that this means trebling training budgets, and sending everyone on courses. Learning organizations have the potential ability to learn from anything that happens within their environment.

PAUSE TO REFLECT

What might this approach to learning encompass?

Now read on.

The Learning Organization

If we consider true learning to be proved when newly acquired attributes (be they skills, knowledge or attitudes) are realized, then some examples of the learning organization in action might be provided when:

- A manufacturer finds out about a planned, competitive product and shortens its own development schedule to pre-empt the competitor
- A public sector agency adapts its appraisal system in response to feedback from the field which suggests it is being applied inconsistently
- A dot.com company extends its catalogue based on the recorded preferences of visitors to its website.

The key point here is that learning does not only happen via structured delivery. It can be derived from almost any circumstance — learning organizations work hard to get their people to recognize when learning has occurred, and when it might occur in future.

In order to establish a culture where people appreciate the ubiquity of learning and development opportunities, several key values need to be in place:

- Learning and development needs to be valued by everyone in the organization, starting from the top of the organization. This means treating learning as an activity with strategic significance: planning and evaluating it alongside mainstream business planning and review; persisting with learning activities (be they R&D programmes, management development or mentoring schemes) even in times of operational or financial constraint; it means talking about learning constantly, at staff meetings, team briefings, in corridors, and across the intranet.
- Learning and development needs to be seen to pay off. The organization, its teams and employees must be clear about what they need to learn and how this will improve performance. Clear, agreed and measurable objectives make the process of evaluating learning and development activities relatively straightforward.
- People should be encouraged to be critical of learning and development. The organization's processes (for planning and reviewing learning) should stimulate employees to view training in the same way as they would appraise a car or discuss a film — as a product from which they expect quality, reliability and even entertainment.
- Learning should be selected for its quality and relevance. A critical audience, clear about what it expects from learning, will be well placed to source suitable provision — as far as possible, people should be enabled to find a learning solution likely to work for them. In some instances this may lead to greater expense on specially commissioned or customized development, but with an appreciation of the total range of learning opportunities, people will often opt for inexpensive and potentially income-generating options such as personal research, or project-based development.

www.universal-manager.co.uk

(4)   Review

Most organizations have numerous review processes: budget reviews, team meetings, annual reports, appraisals, project reporting, etc. The difference in learning organizations is that:

- ☛ There is a will to learn from these processes
- ☛ Open, frank dialogue is encouraged
- ☛ People are not afraid to admit to and reflect on mistakes
- ☛ Conflict, in terms of opposing views, is considered healthy
- ☛ Formal review processes are supplemented (and in some cases replaced) by frequent, informal discussions
- ☛ Self-assessment is often encouraged.

In their struggle to get review processes right, most organizations over-emphasize process design — but it is the behaviour of the people enacting those processes that matters most. Organizational values and norms must free people to approach review in a mature way.

04-5

*Now, Simpkins, this will be your appraisal. I want you to
feel relaxed and free to comment - when I have finished . . .*

The example of the individual review is instructive here. A great number of public and private sector organizations have some form of appraisal or performance review process. A great many of them have expended considerable time and effort on designing the process.

Common concerns in appraisal or performance review design are:

- To ensure that individual performance targets are linked to strategic objectives, and team goals
- Linking personal development to individual performance objectives and collective development plans (e.g. the organizational or team development plan)
- Establishing a fair and transparent system for grading performance
- Linking performance-related pay to grading systems
- Reviewing past performance and development, and planning for future performance and development
- Achieving a balanced perspective on individual performance, perhaps by a combination of self-assessment, peer-review, upward appraisal and 360° degree appraisal
- Trying to ensure that managers and employees go into appraisal fully prepared and ready for a frank exchange of views.

PAUSE TO REFLECT

Think about your own organization's process of appraisal or performance review. Which of the above issues does it seek to address?

Now read on.

It's a fair bet that your organization's process for performance review covers most of the design issues we have itemized, and perhaps more, since our list is not exhaustive. Yet how realistic is it to expect to effectively cover each of those points during a process which, in many workplaces, is essentially an annual two hour discussion, sandwiched between uncomfortable bouts of form-filling? How many appraisal processes facilitate valuable dialogue and lead to genuine performance improvements, or even altered behaviour?

The common tendency in the design and conduct of individual performance review is towards over-complication. Rather than guiding improved performance, appraisal is often perceived as:

- Irrelevant
- An interference
- A waste of time
- Unfair.

It would be a surprise if you had come across none of these charges in your own experience of performance review. But if your experience of appraisal has been more positive, it is likely that the reason had less to do with the process itself than with the people involved. Effective performance review relies on participants who:

- Accept the importance of taking time out to reflect on past performance and plan for the future
- Have the maturity and confidence to give and receive honest feedback
- Are prepared to adapt their behaviour in the light of the insights gained from review.

No process can instil these characteristics into line managers and employees, but through complexity, inconsistency and over-ambition it might stifle any natural inclination they have to engage in effective review. Some of the best processes minimize formality and form-filling (although it is not always possible to do away with them altogether) and concentrate on helping to achieve a strong working relationship between appraiser and appraisee using strategies such as:

- Frequent informal review (perhaps on a monthly basis)
- Removing the 'grading' responsibility from immediate line managers
- Use of psychometric testing to help people identify their own and each other's personal styles
- Aligning performance related pay with team rather than individual performance.

Review, in all its forms, is essential to learning in the workplace — learning organizations seek to remove all the potential inhibitors of open, honest and timely reflection. This, rather than the establishment of elaborate processes, should be the aim of management in a would-be learning organization.

Senge (1990) sees the following as the three main routes by which an organization can evolve into a learning organization and suggests the use of one or a combination of them:

- *Accidental.* Many organizations have become learning organizations without conscious effort or the realization that they were doing so. Independently of the LO concept and principles they have realized that learning is necessary for them to achieve their business goals and have therefore established appropriate systems to facilitate this aim.

- *Subversive*. This organization has realized the likely benefits to be gained from the LO processes but, rather than declaring the aim of becoming a LO, members of the executive quietly get on with the job of introducing necessary processes and systems to introduce the LO culture and thereby enable them to exploit and take advantage of the LO principles.

☞ *Declared.* Here the commitment to become a LO is overt and public and may in the UK, for example, include 'signing up' to the Investors In People initiative and/or introducing other quality systems such as TQM and ISO standards.

With any initiative, once initial enthusiasm has been spent, it is not uncommon to see inertia set in and to allow the initiative to drift into inactivity. How then to sustain the momentum of continuous improvement through learning? Fortunately, experience at LOs has shown that once people begin learning, they find that they enjoy it and can't stop! But this is unlikely to occur if changes have simply been imposed from above.

Another pressure that helps in constant revision of policies and practices is the inexorable increase in the expectation of customers. This is seen in the 'problem' with continuously improving customer service. As has been found in the airline industry, as customers get used to the better service they (a) quickly take for granted the existing level of service (and expect more) and (b) quickly take their custom elsewhere if improvements are not forthcoming.

Learning organization momentum is also likely to be maintained by the organization working towards quality standards such as Investors in People (IIP) and Total Quality Management (TQM — described in Dossier 10 in this series, *Managing for Quality*). Either, or both, of these processes provide good partial frameworks to help the introduction of LO culture to the organization.

The employment of systems thinking is of course essential to understanding how a learning organization functions. Hodgson (1995) quotes Paul Turner of the UK's Trustee Savings Bank:

> *'Models of a learning organization are worthless unless you are prepared to understand the intricacies and complexity of the organization. Changing our culture from that of a traditional bank has meant an acceptance that we can all change. It has been a challenge to simplify the processes and also recognize that implementation requires more sophistication than was needed in the past.'*

Learning organizations, therefore, need new ways of systems thinking. Many organizations see the LO philosophy and methodology as the only way to keep pace with change and to sustain competitive advantage by striving to 'keep one step ahead'. Where resistance is met in the work-force, personnel must be reminded that the LO culture must be to their long-term advantage for continued employment and improved working environment.

CASE STUDY:
SOUTH AFRICAN BREWERIES

South African Breweries (SAB) in 1990, began the deliberate move towards world class manufacturing, best operating practice and international benchmarking. Consultants used an integrated management process to help the 6,000 employees create a sense of community. Key values included customer service, quality, commitment to the environment, respect, equality of opportunity, health and safety and employee development. The last, employee development, was achieved through individual up-skilling and multi-skilling and through team-working, the aim being to improve autonomy and self-management of individuals and teams. Needless to say, demands for training, coaching, and performance management monitoring were considerable. Not all workers were able to cope with the new environment and some redundancies occurred. However, learning processes were made available to help these individuals move on to other employment or to set up their own enterprises.

The ownership of training and learning was encouraged by devolving HR functions to line managers. It thereby became easier to create learning solutions in line with immediate business needs. Where learning off the job was required, learners were able to participate in programmes run by the SAB's corporate university — this was established in partnership with the UK's Herriot Watt and Brunel Universities. In terms of cost, the budget for external training amounted to five per cent of total pay roll and on the job training was subsumed into normal work activities.

But has it worked? Today SAB is both a very low cost producer and a multiple quality award winner! In addition, they have a 20 per cent economic added value — Johan Nel, SAB's HR Director, is reported in *People Management* (30 March 2000) as follows:

'You can't get that without persistently investing in people . . . . There will be no deviating from the kind of intensity and focus we give to people, because we believe it has been the platform of our success over many years. In fact we are likely to increase, rather than decrease, our activity and intent in terms of people management, both locally and from an international perspective.'

04-5

04-6 CURRENT PRACTICE IN LEARNING AND DEVELOPMENT

04-6

04-6 CURRENT PRACTICE IN LEARNING AND DEVELOPMENT

04-6-1 Continuous Professional Development

Our final section takes a critical look at many of the learning methods adopted by organizations today. Although some of the examples referred to are taken from the UK, many of the themes discussed (such as the trend for individuals to take responsibility for their own learning) have a wider resonance.

Learning is all too frequently regarded simply as something done on a course, as an external process, imposed in order to fill a gap in an individual's competences. Under these circumstances, progress is likely to be sporadic, dictated by the availability of suitable provision, the generosity of the training budget and the quality of support from key players in the workplace.

The value of external sources of knowledge and expertise are not to be decried, but they must be seen in the broader context of a range of learning resources and opportunities available to the learner. Generally, the most effective learners are today thought to be those actively engaged in a process of CPD (Continuous Professional Development) and those who take responsibility for their own learning in a practice known as SML (self-managed learning).

Keeping up to date through CPD is seen by many individuals and organizations as an essential prerequisite for success. Indeed, so important is it that evidence of CPD is becoming a standard (or at least desirable) requirement for continued membership of many professional organizations.

Further impetus has come from the decline in job security over the last twenty-five years or so. As traditional industries have died, management structures have flattened and flexible working contracts have become the norm in many sectors; the greatest guarantees of personal prosperity have come to be seen in versatility and continuous development. To some extent, we are all entrepreneurs now, and CPD represents our best shot at continuing to find someone to buy our time.

There are numerous ways in which CPD can occur, some are *ad hoc* and others planned and more formal.

Ad hoc processes include:

☞ Doing the job and reflecting on it
☞ Copying 'best practice' from other practitioners
☞ Responding to needs.

94

Formal CPD may include:

- Identifying development needs (the 'gap analysis' of appraisal)
- Coaching/mentoring/instruction by a trainer, colleague or line manager
- Attendance at conferences and seminars
- The pursuit of formal qualifications.

Where CPD differs from traditional approaches to training and development is in the control it gives the learner, and the responsibility the learner accepts. The mental shift is from training which is 'done to you', to learning which you do yourself.

PAUSE TO REFLECT

This shift from external to personal responsibility and control throws up certain issues to do with work-based learning. What key points occur to you?

Now read on.

There are three key issues related to the philosophy behind CPD and SML which are currently being played out within UK education and training:

04-6

- *Funding*. Who should pay for CPD? The simple answer is: whoever benefits from it, which might include the individual learner, his or her employee and the state. There are initiatives such as the Individual Learning Account scheme which do attempt to combine the interests and financial investment of all three – but indications so far are that people in this country are not yet ready to invest in their own learning.

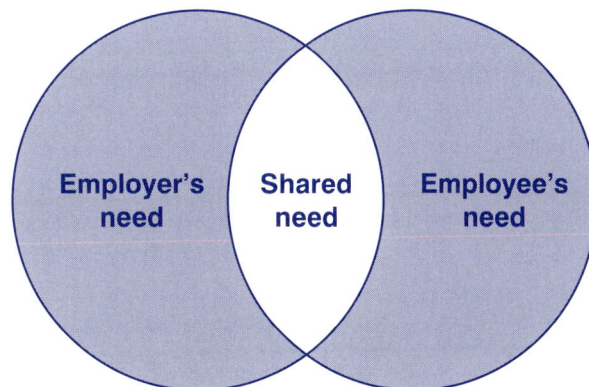

Employer's need | Shared need | Employee's need

☞ *Job-career conflict.* Related to the first issue, this concerns the delicate balance between the employer's development needs and the individual's career plans. Where learning can be identified which marries both sets of requirements, many organizations willingly finance it. But it is probable that the majority of UK employers do not encourage overt career planning at all. Certainly, only a minority of organizations support learning which is not directly job-related, despite the evidence that this type of employee development has a beneficial effect on staff performance and motivation.

☞ *Learning provision.* As demand from individuals for learning provision grows, the calls for more flexible delivery modes will increase. The higher and further education sectors in the UK have been incentivized for some time now to extend and adapt provision to cater for the predicted upturn in demand. Indeed many primary and secondary schools now offer out-of-hours learning provision for adults. In addition, the quality of provision will be subject to increasingly sophisticated customer demand. There are already signs that the supply side is under some strain to meet these growing demands, and one likely implication is that adult learning provision across the UK will be inconsistent in terms of price and quality for some time to come.

04-6-2   Traditional Methods

Since before recorded history, skilled specialists have imparted their knowledge to the next generation. It seems likely that stone-age flint knappers taught their skills to 'apprentices', perhaps within a family group. In this way, skills and knowledge have been disseminated within society, some of this being 'general knowledge' and some being specialized and restricted to family groups. Evidence of this within recorded history is seen in job-related family names such as Cooper (the barrel maker), Fletcher (the arrow maker) and the obvious Smith.

Jackie Butcher
(Counter Assistant)

Dave Shepherd
(Single Parent)

Terry Wacker
(Doorman)

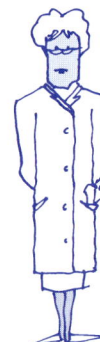

Celia Stirrups
(Midwife)

Related to these traditional routes to learning was the development of various guilds that even today maintain and regulate standards within certain industry sectors (the City and Guilds of London Institute awarding body is a descendant of the guilds movement). Based on the model of the guilds, which were craft orientated, there have now developed many professional bodies such as the Institute of Management and the Chartered Institute of Personnel and Development that are also concerned with the maintenance of standards and like to see evidence of CPD amongst their members.

(1) Learning on the job

With the advent of the Industrial Revolution in the mid-1700s, a wider range of very specialized jobs developed and with them the need for very skilled individuals. Training for these jobs was carried out 'on the job' and, in many industries, formal contracts (indentures) were drawn up between the apprentice and the master craftsman who was responsible for their training.

Traditionally, apprenticeships were time-serving training with no formal qualifications being offered. However, in the 1900s it became increasingly common in the UK for apprentices to undertake a 'day release' technical college course, leading to City and Guilds (or similar) vocational qualifications. Since the mid-1980s, both on-the-job and off-the-job training has become more structured with the emphasis being on government funded schemes leading to NVQs (National Vocational Qualifications) and SVQs (Scottish Vocational Qualifications).

In contrast to the disjunction of 'work' and 'training', the Modern Apprenticeship and the National Traineeship schemes for young people attempt (with varying degrees of success) to integrate the two processes. An 'off-the-job' training programme leading towards formal vocational qualifications (normally specified as an S/NVQ) is provided and this is run in parallel with 'on-the-job training'.

04-6

(2) Learning off the job

During the last 50 years it has become increasingly common for structured training to take place and a parallel course leading to a recognized qualification to be taken. In the UK, these day release courses (until the 1990s) typically ran from September to June and took anything from one to three years of study with a day a week, or a day plus an evening, being spent at an institution in which non-differentiated traditional teaching or lecturing was the norm. Although the use of the past tense in the previous sentence suggests that things are no longer done this way, it would be more accurate to say that while intentions (on the part of funding bodies and learning providers) have changed, the majority of organized off-the-job learning still happens in this way.

The Learning Organization

In addition to these longer courses a huge variety of courses is available from a range of providers and these are examined below.

ACTIVITY 13

What, from your own organization's perspective, are the comparative benefits and drawbacks of on- and off-the-job learning?

	Benefits	Drawbacks
On-job		
Off-job		

Compare your response with ours in the commentary in Appendix 1.

(3) Vocational qualifications

In the late 1980s, Western governments — concerned about the rapid development in Far East economies — began to develop a philosophy of competitiveness. Over the last fifteen years in the UK, no area of government activity has been exempt from the influence of 'competition-based reform', and education and training has probably been one of the areas most affected.

In essence, the idea of competitiveness says that:

☛ In order to catch up with, maintain parity with or stay ahead of competitive nations, our economy and our infrastructure must be designed to reduce inefficiencies and improve individual performance.

☛ Traditional structures and attitudes are holding us back — for instance, technical crafts tend to suffer from skill shortage in the UK. One reason often given is the comparatively low status afforded to engineers and technicians in this country, where our European counterparts equate engineering with medicine and law.

☛ Systems, perceptions and practices need to change now in order to remain competitive in future.

ACTIVITY 14

Note down three significant changes that have occurred in education over the last fifteen to twenty years. To what extent are they linked to the drive for competitiveness?

Compare your response with ours in the commentary in Appendix 1.

From the mid-1980s a new national framework of vocational education based on S/NVQ (Scottish/National Vocational Qualification) standards has been developed. These qualifications (unlike traditional qualifications, which are defined in terms of a teaching syllabus) are based on 'learning outcomes'. As such, they do not define the content of training course but rather the outcomes from such a programme.

04-6

At the same time as the introduction and development of S/NVQs, 'new' funding systems for further education colleges and other training providers have been introduced, forcing them to become more flexible and responsive to client needs. The distinction between polytechnics and universities was removed in the late-1980s as part of a trend to 'upgrade' vocational education — the proportion of vocational courses now offered by universities has dramatically increased over the last ten years. Many providers now offer flexible forms of learning delivery, such as 'roll-on, roll-off' programmes. However, the content and pace still tend to be determined by the institution and the links between external provision and work-based application of learning are still generally weak.

Formerly seen as the preserve of further education, many private providers and universities now offer short-course and day-release programmes of great variety. The further education sector is thus increasingly competitive and despite the huge number of 'off-the-shelf' training packages, 'bespoke' programmes designed around client requirements are now increasingly commonplace.

(4) Short courses

The realization by users and providers of education and training that cost-effectiveness is a major factor in the choice of programmes has driven the development of the very lucrative short course market. Huge numbers of courses are available from public, private and in-house training providers — they may be as short as an hour or so, or as long as several weeks duration. The short courses can be delivered at the provider's premises or on site. Most are 'packages' that range from the generic (perhaps covering general skills of management or IT packages) to the highly specific (perhaps manufacturer's training in the correct use of a piece of machinery).

The obvious advantage of short courses for employed people is that they reduce the amount of downtime associated with learning.

04-6-3   Non-traditional Methods

Typically in SML (self-managed learning) the learner occupies centre stage with providers and facilitators working to enable the learning processes to occur with maximum efficiency. With help and guidance (perhaps from a work-based mentor or coach), the person engaged in SML defines their learning aims and objectives in a form of learning plan or contract.

Constable (2000) suggests a number of questions to help the learner to focus on devising an individual development plan. The questions are equally applicable to the broader processes of CPD and the list can be expanded through discussion with an appraiser or through group work. The questions may include an evaluation of individual roles and needs such as:

- How do I want to develop my role in the organization?
- In what direction do I perceive my developmental/career path?
- How does this equate with organizational needs/prospects?
- What skills/attributes/competences will I need to fulfil this role?
- How do my present skill/attributes/competences compare with those required?
- In the light of the above, where are the gaps and what do I need to learn?

The focus provided by the learning contract increases the likelihood of success in the CPD/SML processes.

SML 'tools' bring together a menu of different approaches and makes these accessible to the learner. The following outlines the main features of some different learning approaches that can be used in CPD and are subsumed into SML.

(1) Open and distance learning

Perhaps the most widely known type of non-traditional and independent study route is through *open learning* in which an external organization provides structured learning materials and periodic visits are made by the learner to a learning centre for group meetings or meetings with a mentor or tutor. The best known and internationally famous example of such a provider is the Open University. Advantages of open learning are perceived to include:

- Organizational systems can be arranged to allow large numbers of learners to work simultaneously on a given programme
- The programmes are relatively flexible, allowing people to work at their own pace
- Learners fit the programme into their lifestyle and choose where, when and how to study
- This type of learning usually costs less than personal delivery.

Even so, there are a number of drawbacks to open learning and these include:

- The tendency for employers to purchase standard packages that may have only a limited relationship with the learner's specific, and probably work-related, requirements.
- The pace is dictated to some extent by deadlines for assessed work, tutorial sessions and examination schedules.
- Due to its solitary nature, there is a phenomenon known as 'the loneliness of the open/distance learner' in which the learner may miss the personal contact with fellow students and tutors and the energizing stimulation of live debate.

04-6

- The provider can seem remote and impersonal. (But the occasional group and one-to-one tutorials and the use of the Internet can help to overcome these problems.)

A variant on open learning is *distance learning*. This differs from open learning in the nature and frequency of contact with the provider. Indeed, with properly structured, self-contained materials, there may be no direct contact with the provider at all.

The advantages and disadvantages of distance learning are very similar to those of open learning, with the drawback of 'loneliness' being even more marked.

(2) Computer-based learning

Computer-based learning has been around for longer than is generally thought (some quite sophisticated programmes had already been developed by 1980) but it was not until fairly recently that it was seen as a viable, accessible medium for delivering learning on a wide variety of topics. The breakthrough came courtesy of the internet, but there is still uncertainty over the practicality and effectiveness of learning delivered over the web.

Although there are many fine distinctions between different types of computer-based learning, it is now reasonable to concentrate on two main variants:

- ☛ *Computer-based training (CBT)* — where typically the programme will be stored on a CD-ROM containing all the necessary content and media
- ☛ *On-line learning* — where the materials are held on the server of the provider or an ISP (Internet Service Provider).

With CBT, provided your computing system meets the programme's specified requirements, working through a learning programme is straightforward — all the text, graphics and other media will run on demand as long as the material has been properly coded. It's a format ideal for simulation, certain forms of practical and knowledge testing, scenario building and demonstrations. The main drawbacks with CBT are the isolation factor already described in relation to open learning, and price. CBT is very expensive to design and programme, which means that unless the material is a guaranteed best seller (e.g. an IT or keyboard title) it tends not be priced to appeal to the individual consumer, and many organizations think twice about purchasing expensive programmes with their associated license and maintenance costs.

On-line learning promised to overcome the price hurdle — subscription charging allows a modular, pay as you learn approach . . .

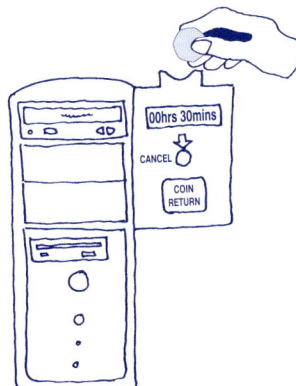

. . . and it also encourages more critical selection of learning materials. In addition, web-based learning enables us to plug into a network of other learners via forums, discussion groups and bulletin boards, and can put learners in touch with tutors and expert practitioners. So far though, there is not much evidence of the promised take-off of on-line delivery, not even in the US where 90% of large firms claim to be delivering learning across corporate intranets (there is a strong suspicion that this figure includes many non-interactive forms of delivery). There are three main reasons for this hiatus:

☛ *Download times.* In the UK the average modem connection speed is still 56k — downloading large or complex graphics or photographs, movies or audio clips (indeed all the media that can make computer-based learning exciting and stimulating) is often a slow process. Too slow for most of us, particularly when we are trying to achieve a relaxed state of learning concentration. This aspect of web-based learning compares unfavourably with CBT, but it is thought that the next generation of internet connections will make light of the problem.

☛ *Workstation limitations.* Quite simply, most working adults today are not comfortable learning from a VDU. Apart from the isolation, there is the physical discomfort to contend with — eye strain, backache and so on.

☛ *Supply limitations*. Computer-based learning of both kinds (CBT and on-line) looks likely to remain expensive to develop for some time to come. A major factor here is the complexity of managing a computer-based learning development project: it requires design skills, programming skills, subject expertise and project management capability. At present, there are not enough organizations and not enough individuals with the competence to develop computer-based learning material to a consistently high standard.

04-6

There is little doubt that the technical limitations will be overcome, and the required skills base will grow enormously over the next few years — who knows, we may even evolve so that the workstation becomes our natural environment! In the short term, however, computer-based learning is best approached as an exciting, but specialized, format which needs to be supported by other learning media, and preferably human interaction.

04-6-4   Action Learning

In this section our use of the term 'action learning' is broad, and concerns any situation where people:

- Learn from their own experience or their own efforts in their work roles
- Reflect on what they have learned.

But in fact there is a more correct interpretation of the practice of action learning, derived from the work of Reg Revans (1982), which it will be useful to summarize here.

Revans simplified his theory of action learning thus:

$$L = P + Q$$

Where   L is learning
P is 'programmed' knowledge, i.e. known and perhaps published concepts and data
Q is 'questioning' insight, clarifying the nature of a problem by intelligent investigation.

Pure action learning is therefore applicable to problems — situations where the best solution is not known or accessible to those involved. It works by a process of first asking questions to clarify the exact nature of the problem, then identifying possible solutions and finally taking action. But Revans adds a fourth stage — reflection, to identify exactly what has been learned, internalize the lessons and plan to take appropriate action in future, even in different situations.

The chief qualities needed to practise effective action learning are similar to those cultural characteristics discussed in Section 04-5:

- Clear-sighted curiosity
- Creativity to generate potential solutions
- The confidence (and support) to take risks
- A predisposition towards learning from experience.

It is unusual to find all these qualities embodied in the same manager, and partly for this reason, pure action learning tends to be conducted within project or task groups.

Our own interpretation of action learning focuses on the reflective element of the process, the deliberate attempt to capitalize on individual and collective experience.

PAUSE TO REFLECT

What would you identify as the advantages of experience as a source of learning, when compared with structured training? And what about the drawbacks?

Now read on.

'Mining' experience will almost always cost less than structured training: it is in great supply, accumulating naturally on an everyday basis. Experience is never artificial or isolated from the actual work situation. By definition, it is the consequence of the activity which occurs when staff carry out their normal work roles. Its relevance is unquestionable. Any learning triggered by experience is highly likely to be applicable to the work situation from which it arose.

The two main potential drawbacks with experience-based learning are that:

- It can tend to promote insularity
- It is necessarily limited to historical events.

For the remainder of this section we will consider four approaches to organizational learning which attempt to capitalize on existing experience, relationships and processes in the workplace. The underlying principle is that effective learning does not rely solely on structured or external provision; it can be achieved in the course of normal work activities.

04-6

(1) Knowledge Transfer

Despite the semi-technological mystique surrounding the discipline of knowledge management, at its heart is a simple and compelling idea. All individuals and hence all teams and organizations contain a great deal of tacit knowledge, i.e. knowledge which is locked up in people's minds. Knowledge management (KM) seeks to convert tacit into explicit knowledge, accessible to everyone in the organization who can benefit from it.

Of course not all tacit knowledge is useful to others, and not everyone needs to have knowledge which might be useful to only a few. So effective knowledge management systems (KMS) seek to identify and tap into useful tacit knowledge, and then route it to those who need it. A common example occurs with customer contact databases: perhaps everyone in the organization has access to the data, but different groups need it for different reasons — the processes used to convert the raw data into useful information (such as sales reports and forecasts, or mailing lists) are in effect the routes by which the data is converted into explicit knowledge.

In fact the start of the conversion occurs when the data is input or updated by staff in contact with customers.

A well known KMS has been implemented at Ford — it enables employees who have discovered efficiency or quality improvement measures to input the details on a database, and share their experience with Ford units around the world. This and other KM case studies are described in Dossier 05 of this series *Managing for Knowledge*.

There is no doubt that Information Communications Technology is a great enabler of knowledge transfer, but, of course, it is only as effective as those who use it to seek out and share experience. As with organizational learning, effective knowledge management relies on the curiosity and commitment of people.

(2) Competitive Intelligence (CI)

CI is one way businesses actively try to add to corporate knowledge, but it is knowledge of a specific kind: keen awareness of competitors' organizations, circumstances and plans. Not to be confused with industrial espionage, CI is the legitimate, structured process of gleaning as much useful intelligence about competitors as can be found in the public domain.

ACTION ACTIVITY 15

What potential sources of competitive intelligence does your organization make use of?

Compare your response with our commentary in Appendix 1.

Some organizations choose to make a specialism of competitive intelligence, either retaining research firms to investigate competitors, or in some cases employing people full time to do that work. But in small and medium sized enterprises, without the resources to invest seriously in CI, there is a great deal that the organization can learn from those staff who are in most frequent contact with customers, suppliers and distributors. As sources of information about market conditions, prospects and developments, these are hard to beat, but very few businesses systematically attempt to use them.

(3)   Performance Review

In Section 04-5, we described the part that effective review can play in organizational learning, emphasizing in particular the barriers that complex, over-ambitious processes can place in the way of constructive, honest dialogue.

Whether the subject of the review is corporate financial performance, a sales team's progress towards targets, or an individual's performance at work over the last twelve months, review meetings represent a precious opportunity for reflection and, in some cases, for joint problem solving. Yet so often these sessions are characterized by:

- The confrontational and defensive roles adopted by participants
- Absenteeism or postponement
- Primacy of the timetable over the attainment of useful conclusions
- Limited opportunity for discussion of underlying issues.

If such occasions are not suitable for tackling problems and reflecting on experience, when does this happen? For a great many organizations, the unavoidable response is: not at all.

(4)   Coaching and Mentoring

Increasingly, coaching and mentoring skills are seen as indispensable to the manager with line responsibility. Effectively deployed they can provide an excellent lubricant for the machinery of a learning organization. Deployment is the key word, because none of the skills required to act as coach or mentor should be unfamiliar to any manager. Questioning, listing, suggesting, problem solving, advocating — these are all routine communication skills. With coaching and mentoring, the main trick is to use them at the right time, and in a manner appropriate to the situation.

Coaching

ACTION ACTIVITY 16

The illustration above shows a variety of coaching styles that may be adopted depending on the situation.

Think about a specific situation where you were trying to bring the best out of someone (it should preferably be a work-based example).

With your example in mind, try to identify which coaching style(s) you adopted in that situation and how it influenced the eventual outcome.

Now read on.

Coaching is about getting the best performance out of people, using the most appropriate means. In other words, it is important to adopt a suitable style. In fact it may be necessary to adopt a range of different styles over the course of a relationship.

Here is a brief summary of how each of the coaching styles on our continuum works in practice.

☞   *Mirror* — observes and describes performance back to subject, leaving them to reach their own conclusions.

☞   *Conscience* — asks probing, often awkward questions, prompting subject to appropriate conclusions about current performance.

☞   *Ideas generator* — helps subject come up with optional courses of action, assists them with selecting and refining suitable options. Less directive is the 'sounding board' for the subject's own ideas.

☞   *Joint problem solver* — helps subject analyse and think though problems. Often participates in decision making.

☞   *Trainer* — explains, demonstrates, tests and assesses as appropriate.

www.universal-manager.co.uk

☛ *Expert* — may simply provide information or guidance, but is more often the authoritative source on the right or best way.

The prevailing wisdom is that coaches should always aim, over time, towards a less directive relationship with their subject. In the formula of Tim Galwey — one of the founders of coaching, quoted in Parsloe (2000):

'Performance = Potential – Interference'.

However, in practice, there will always be certain people and certain times which call for the hands-on approach.

Mentoring

The many different interpretations of the roles of coach and mentor tend to blur distinctions between them. But it is possible to identify some important differences, which suggest that:

☛ The same person should not take on both roles for the same person
☛ It might be overkill, particularly in a small organization, to try to implement coaching and mentoring schemes simultaneously.

The following table illustrates some of the key divergences between the roles of mentor and coach.

04-6

Coaching vs Mentoring

Coaches	Mentors
☛ Tend to be result-oriented ☛ Usually have a practical focus ☛ Operate on a needs basis, but are usually in constant contact ☛ Tend to be senior people with more extensive experience (not necessarily stronger performers)	☛ Typically aim to support long-term growth ☛ Often offer or exchange wisdom ☛ May be remote, but often stay with the subject for longer ☛ Might be a role model, independent observer or peer

In the same way that effective coaches need to be able to adopt a range of different approaches as befits the situation, there is some variety in the possible approaches to mentoring. But here it is perhaps most important to get the purpose, the process and the participants right (with coaching this is usually straightforward — line manager develops employee). We look in more depth at coaching and mentoring relationships in Dossier 11 — *Business Relationships*.

Before we close this dossier with a final, summative exercise, here are three varied summary case studies on mentoring.

(1)   Roger Enrico, CEO of **Pepsico**, set up a mentoring scheme, where at one stage he was devoting half his time to developing the company's up and coming young executives. At organized retreats he arranged for selected participants to each bring a big idea for business development. Over time, with Enrico personally mentoring each one, the future stars of the organization refined and implemented their projects. *Here mentoring is used to groom talent and develop the business.*

(2)   **KPMG** has a strong and elaborate counselling system tied into the accountancy qualifications framework. There are counselling partners charged with monitoring the long term development of employees; counselling managers who meet employees every 6 – 12 months to review performance and development; and line managers with day to day responsibility for individuals, who will agree objectives for and review performance on each assignment the employee undertakes. KPMG also has a buddy system for new recruits who can stay with a person for several years. *Mentoring here is an integral part of a number of relationships designed together to develop competence and confidence, improve performance and support career growth.*

(3)   **IBM** implemented a formal mentoring programme in 1995 across its North America sales and services division. They describe the scheme as a contract between organization and employee: *IBM gets enhanced core competencies, while the participating employees get greater 'career resilience'.* Mentors and their protégés are not connected by the direct line of reporting — sometimes mentors have to say hard things that the protégé might not like to hear.

04-6-5   Summary of Learning

In the spirit of action learning, we will close this dossier with an exercise designed to help you reflect on what you have learned from your study of *The Learning Organization*, and how you might apply it within your work role.

![Action icon] **ACTIVITY 17**

From the checklist below pick out the three topics from this dossier which struck you as having most to offer you and your organization. Make a note of some specific ways you might apply your learning on these topics, and comment on the two or three key things you will need to do to make it happen.

Topics	How you might apply them	Making it happen
Double loop learning (04-1-2) Personal mastery (04-1-2) Mental models (04-1-2) Shared vision (04-1-2) Team learning (04-1-2) Systems thinking (04-1-2) Adult learning (04-2-1) Experiential learning (04-2-1) Learning styles (04-2-1) Multiple intelligences (04-2-2) Emotional intelligence (04-2-2) Neuro-linguistic programming (04-2-2) Collective learning strategies (04-2-3) Strategic learning (04-3-1) Learning evaluation (04-3-2) Learning needs analysis (04-4-1) Competences (04-4-2) Developing a learning culture (04-5) Traditional learning methods (04-6-2) Open and distance learning (04-6-3) Computer-based learning (04-6-3) Action learning (04-6-4) Knowledge transfer (04-6-4) Competitive Intelligence (04-6-4) Coaching (04-6-4) Mentoring (04-6-4)		

04-6

This is the end of Dossier 04.

APPENDIX 1

COMMENTARY ON ACTIVITIES

Activity 2

Here are some suggested approaches for removing the five barriers identified in the exercise:

(1) *Lack of awareness*. The obvious tactic here is to communicate, communicate, communicate! Many messages in organizations need to be repeated, reiterated and reinforced: this means sending out the same message at different times, and using different formats (e.g. notice boards, memos, e-mail, staff meetings, etc.). But perhaps more effective would be to try and instil an awareness of learning opportunities through key organizational processes like induction, performance review, even pay day (which some firms use for important communications).

(2) *Lack of desire*. Some people will respond best when they are shown that it is in their material interest to take up learning; others will be influenced by senior figures or peers; while there are some people who may need to be told fairly forcefully that learning is an integral part of the job. Key to adopting the right persuasive tactic will be to try and identify the source of the employee's reluctance. For instance, if a poor track record in education is the problem, a sensible approach might be to outline all the available learning options, stressing the non-academic routes.

(3) *Lack of suitable provision*. Assuming that there is relevant provision available but that it isn't convenient for the employee and/or the organization, some sort of compromise might need to be struck, perhaps to compensate or incentivize the employee for after-hours learning. Or it may be necessary to negotiate with a learning provider to deliver in the manner required. If there simply is no relevant provision, it might well be necessary for the organization to commission something suitable.

(4) *Cost*. The first point here is to attempt to quantify the value of the proposed learning to the organization (and employee). Usually the potential value far outweighs the cost — if it doesn't, you should question the relevance of the learning. At the same time, there are often ways of reducing learning costs, either by negotiation with the provider, application to local or national government learning support schemes (such as Individual Learning Accounts), or by making it a condition that the employee makes some financial contribution (this often does wonders for motivation to stick with the programme!).

(5) *Inconvenience.* The source of the inconvenience needs to be identified before any solution can be determined. If it is to do with time or resourcing, often the employer can help. Personal difficulties are trickier, but a line manager who has a good relationship with employees might be able to help arrive at a solution.

Activity 3

(1) *Inappropriate method.* In order to avoid learning delivery by inappropriate methods, it often helps to have an idea of the employee's preferred learning style (discussed later in Section 04-2-1). Line managers may need to help employees think about what types of learning they respond to best and which types have proved ineffective in the past.

(2) *Inappropriate level.* Any significant learning activity or event should be defined in terms of who should take part, and what entry requirements there are (if any). A further check on learning at the wrong level should be some form of initial assessment (generally only undertaken for learning programmes lasting several months or longer) — this may go as far as identifying the learners current level of competency, and can be used to map out a personal development plan.

(3) *Insufficient relevance.* In selecting learning activities, employers (and their managers) need to be fussy and perhaps ask awkward questions such as 'why do my people have to attend the whole programme when only the morning of Day 4 affects us?'. At the same time, learners are not always quick to spot the relevance of certain learning and many will benefit from a pre-activity briefing to clarify precisely their expectations.

(4) *Lack of support.* The short answer here is — provide the necessary support. It could be as simple as taking a genuine interest, and not waiting until annual appraisal to ask how a training course went. Equally it might involve the manager in helping the employee make certain arrangements to facilitate the learning process, such as the use of certain resources or a degree of flexibility on time-keeping. If the learning is of value to the organisation, line manager support will be paid back in improved performance.

(5) *Lack of tangible result.* This barrier might apply in particular to those learners who prefer action-centred, practical learning activities. As far as possible, their learning activities should be selected to match that pre-disposition. In designing learning activities and materials it is always a good idea, no matter what the audience, to give people an early chance to do something practical.

114

Activity 4

MI	Personal characteristics	Value to LO
Interpersonal Intelligence	Sensitive to others and their views. Relates well to others and has lots of friends. Learns well through group work.	'Reads' the thought processes of others — teamworker. Good mediation and negotiation skills. Market research/customer care.
Intra-personal Intelligence	Has good self-knowledge and uses this to operate effectively in life/work. Is reflective, perhaps introspective. Aware of what drives and motivates self — perhaps self-sufficient. Learns alone with individual projects.	High order of thinking and reasoning. Self motivating.
Verbal/ Linguistic Intelligence	Enjoys the use and power of language and good conversation. Enjoys reading/writing. Enjoys 'play on words'. Learns by hearing/saying.	Communicator/negotiator/teacher. Power of persuasion/marketing/ selling. Copywriting. Law/contracts.
Logical/ Mathematical Intelligence	Good with numbers/maths/algebra/ science and abstract patterns. Good spatial abilities. Learns by categorizing and classifying/ looks for abstract patterns and relationships.	Logical and deductive reasoning. Science & scientific investigative methods/engineering/technology/ ICT. Sees relationships and links. Modelling scenarios. Accounting.
Visual/ Spatial Intelligence	Discerning of patterns and colours. May have drawing & design skills. Good map/plan reader. Understands plans easily. Learns by visualization and imagery.	Scenario visualizations. 2-D and 3-D design interests. Graphics and visualizations.
Body/ Kinaesthetic Intelligence	Good mind body connectivity/physical control/spatial abilities. Enjoys physical activities, sports, etc. Good spatial abilities. Learns through movement and use of bodily sensations.	Probably a 'doer'. Probably good with tools/manual-skills/ crafts person. Reads body language — negotiation/ sales. Uses drama to good effect.
Musical/ Rhythmic Intelligence	Musical — sings and whistles in tune. Rhythmical/responsive to music. Enjoys music and perhaps music making. Learns through rhythm/music/melody.	Immediate value is dependent on the organization — essential, for example, in the music industry. Sensitive to voice/tone/timbre.

Activity 8

Your response may have mentioned remote or self-managed learning methods such as:

- Open learning
- Reading
- Research
- Watching a video
- Taking an on-line learning module.

But there are many other ways of acquiring new skills or knowledge such as:

- Shadowing or observing others
- Attending conferences, seminars, network events, etc.
- One-to-one or group discussions
- Carrying out projects
- Job swaps or secondments.

Although our list of learning methods is growing, none of those mentioned so far really gets to the heart of how learning occurs. Some of the most powerful learning any of us experiences is delivered in situations which are harder to categorize (and hence harder to plan), such as when:

- We fail or witness failure at first hand
- We succeed or witness success at first hand
- We are prompted to reflect on our experience by a painful, humiliating, exhilarating or otherwise memorable experience
- We are immersed in a situation which leaves us no choice but to adapt (immersion in a foreign culture for instance is considered to be by far the best way of learning a foreign language)
- We make accidental discoveries.

Activity 9

Level	Current position	Gap	Desired destination
Organization	- Definition of core competencies - Internal review - External review		- Strategic objectives/ priorities - Quality models

Level	Current position	Gap	Desired destination
Team/Department/ Unit	☞ Critical incident analysis ☞ Repertory grid ☞ Internal review (e.g. team discussion) ☞ External review (e.g. cross departmental discussion) ☞ Historical performance analysis		☞ Team objectives and action plans ☞ Competence frameworks (particularly for common functional needs) ☞ Collective development goals
Individual	☞ Self-assessment ☞ One-to-one appraisal ☞ 360° appraisal or other feedback from peers		☞ Individual performance objectives ☞ Competence frameworks (and linked career plans) ☞ Job descriptions

Activity 10

According to Robert Wood and Tim Payne (1998), the twelve competences most commonly adopted by UK organizations are:

☞ Communication
☞ Achievement/results orientation
☞ Customer focus
☞ Teamwork
☞ Leadership
☞ Planning and organizing
☞ Commercial/business awareness
☞ Flexibility/adaptability
☞ Developing others
☞ Problem solving
☞ Analytical thinking
☞ Building relationships.

Activity 12

Ideally, an organization wishing to encourage leadership at every level should provide an information and development programme based upon a clear identification of the behaviour expected of the new leaders. This would detail:

☞ New responsibilities
☞ Key competences
☞ New areas of authority.

Identification of the competences ought preferably to involve the new leaders as well as some experienced people, and should focus on:

- The behaviour expected of excellent performers
- The potential barriers to success
- Strategies for overcoming the barriers.

It would be important that the development offered learners the opportunity to practice (without full responsibility) and gave access to coaching or mentoring from experienced practitioners.

Reward and recognition would play an important role. The idea would not be simply to reward people for taking on greater responsibility or authority, but to alter the existing reward structure so that it did not encourage reversion to old work practices, and so that it did encourage high levels of performance in the new role. Recognition would take the form of constructive, specific and timely feedback.

Finally, in ideal circumstances, there would be a phased transition allowing the new leaders to ease into the role.

Activity 13

You may have suggested benefits and drawbacks similar to these:

	Benefits	**Drawbacks**
On-job	- Reduces downtime - Direct relevance - Opportunities for skills application - Easy to involve teams, cohorts or cross-departmental groups	- Insularity - Environment may seem stale, not conducive to learning - Lack of validation - May not be delivered by expert trainer
Off-job	- Might expose learner to useful external influences - Refreshes learner - Likely to lead to a qualification - Expertise of instructional provider	- Requires job cover - Relevance uncertain - May take place in an unrepresentative environment - Learner will probably attend in isolation

www.universal-manager.co.uk

Activity 14

Here are four examples of the significant change that has occurred in the provision of education and training in the UK over the last twenty years:

☞ Introduction of the national curriculum. The definition of minimum standards for school age pupils was intended to drive up attainment levels, particularly in the key areas of literacy, numeracy and science.

☞ Development of the NVQ framework. NVQs were originally proposed as the solution to many of industry's capability problems: reducing training costs, providing national standards of competence, and mapping out the required skills and knowledge for a range of occupational areas with no uniform criteria.

☞ Introduction of performance review for teachers. This recent initiative, not well received by teachers or their unions, was intended to introduce a business-like approach to performance management skills, and thus ensure greater effectiveness within the profession.

☞ Launch of the University for Industry (UfI). This government-backed agency was launched in 1999 to stimulate the supply and take-up of computer-based and on-line learning. The UK government's pre-occupation with Information Communications Technology is well known, and UfI is part of a major series of initiatives designed to ensure prominence in future global commerce, particularly e-commerce.

These four examples serve to demonstrate the strong link between continuous reform of UK education and training, and the desire to achieve and sustain competitiveness for our economy.

Activity 15

It is surprising how much information other organizations do put into the public domain. You might have identified the following potential sources of competitive intelligence:

☞ In certain circumstances there may be a legal requirement to 'go public' as with the official notice that must be given of construction plans (a clear sign of expansion)

☞ Many organizations publish detailed annual reviews and accounts, either on paper, on websites or both

☞ Promotional information such as advertisements and brochures will describe competing ranges, and perhaps more importantly, the benefits your competitors are offering customers

☞ Of course any product is a potential source of competitive intelligence, particularly when it can be studied and 'reverse engineered' to see how it has been put together

☞ In addition to official registrations with UK Companies House, a great many businesses are featured in specialist directories.

APPENDIX 2

USEFUL RESOURCES

Bibliography/Texts

Other (linked or relevant) Universal Manager dossiers:
    Dossier 05:   *Managing for Knowledge*
    Dossier 14:   *21st Century Communication*

d'Ambra (1999), *Measure Your EQ Factor*, Foulsham.

C Argyris (1977), 'Double Loop Learning in Organizations', *Harvard Business Review*, Sept – Oct.

C Argyris (1992), *On Organizational Learning*, Blackwell.

C Argyris (1993), *Knowledge for Action*, Jossey-Brass.

C Argyris, D A Schön (1996), *Organizational Learning II*, Addison-Wesley Publishing.

T Armstrong (1993), *Seven Kinds of Smart*, Plume.

G Azzopardi (2000*), IQ May Get You a Job; EQ Will Get You Promoted*, Foulsham.

R Bandler and J Grindler (1996), *Frogs into Princes*, Eden Grove Editions.

R Boyzatis (1982), *The Competent Manager*, John Wiley.

J Carroll (1990), *The Nurnberg Funnel*, MIT Press.

A Constable (1995), 'Self-managed Learning' in *The Financial Times Handbook of Management*, (ed. S Crainer), Pitmans.

R Cooper & A Sawaf (1998), *Executive EQ*, Orion Business.

K P Cross (1981), *Adults as Learners*, San Francisco: Jossey-Bass.

N Dixon (1999) *The Organizational Learning Cycle: How We Can Learn Collectively*, Gower Publishing.

N Dixon (2000), *Common Knowledge: How Companies Thrive by Sharing What They Know*, HBS Press.

Fiol & Lyles, 'Organizational Learning', *Academy of Management Review*, October 1985.

R Gagné (1977), *The Conditions of Learning*, Rhinehart & Wilson.

H Gardner (1993), *Frames of Mind*, Fontana.

H Gardner (2000), *Intelligence Reframed: Multiple Intelligences for the 21st Century*, Basic Books.

D Garvin (1993), 'Building a Learning Organization', *Harvard Business Review*, July – Aug.

D Goleman, (1996), *Emotional Intelligence*, Bloomsbury Publishing.

D Goleman (1998), *Working With Emotional Intelligence*, Bloomsbury Publishing.

C Harris, (1999*), NLP: An Introductory Guide to the Art and Science of Excellence*, Element Books.

P Hodgson (1995), 'The Learning Organization' in *The Financial Times Handbook of Management*, (ed. S Crainer), Pitmans.

R M Kanter (1983), *The Change Masters*, International Thomson Business Press.

D Kolb (1984), *Experiential Learning*, Prentice Hall.

Levitt & March (1988), 'Organizational Learning', *American Review of Sociology*.

J Mayer, M DiPaolo, P Salovey (1990), 'Perceiving Affective Content in Ambiguous Visual Stimuli', *Journal of Personality Assessment*, **54**, 722 – 781.

H Mintzberg (1994), *The Rise and Fall of Strategic Planning*, Financial Times-Prentice Hall.

A Mumford (1986), *Handbook of Management Development*, Gower.

R Nevans (1982), *The Original Growth of Action Learning*, Chartwell Bratt.

E Parsloe, M Wray (2000), *Coaching and Mentoring*, Kogan Page.

M Pedler and K Aspinall (1998), *A Concise Guide to the Learning Organization*, Nemos & Crane.

A Pettigrew and R Whipp (1991), *Managing Change for Competitive Skills*, Blackwell.

C Rogers (1994), *Freedom to Learn*, Merrill/Macmillan.

D Ryback, (1997), *Putting Emotional Intelligence to Work: Successful Leadership is More Than IQ*, Butterworth Heinemann.

P Salovey and J Mayer (1990), 'Emotional Intelligence', *Imagination, Cognition and Personality*, **9**, 185 – 211.

P Salovey and D Sluyter (1997), *Emotional Development and Emotional Intelligence*, Basic Books.

D Schön (1987), *Educating the Reflective Practitioner*, Jossey-Bass.

P M Senge (1999), *The Dance of Change*, Nicholas Brealey.

P M Senge (1993), *The Fifth Discipline*, Century Arrow (Business).

P M Senge, A Kleiner, C Roberts, R Ross, B Smith (1994), *The Fifth Discipline Fieldbook*, Nicholas Brealey Publishing.

H Weisinger (1997), *Emotional Intelligence at Work: The Untapped Edge for Success*, Jossey-Bass.

Useful Websites

Should you find that any of the links below is not working, check with the Universal Manager site (www.universal-manager.co.uk) where links are updated frequently.

Links for Learning and Learning Organizations

www.learning-org.com (*hosts a discussion group dedicated to the learning organization.*)
www.fieldbook.com/main.html
www.sol-ne.org (*site for The Society for Organizational Learning.*)
http://educ.queensu.ca/~russellt/schon87.htm (*lecture given by Donald Schön*)
http://world.std.com/~lo/WhyLO.html
www.peterhoney.com (*influential UK thinker on learning theory and practice.*)
http://sdnhq.undp.org/mirrors/as/india/
www.actionscience.com/actinq.htm
www.eclo.org/conferences/1997/a02.htm
http://www.iipuk.co.uk

Links to sites on intelligence

www.sciam.com/speicalissues/1198intelligence/1198gottfred.html
www.bhs.mq.edu.au/~tbates104/IQ_history

Links to sites on Multiple Intelligence

www.harding.edu/~cbr/midemo/defi.html

Links to sites on Emotional Intelligence

http://eqi.org/salovey.htm
http://eqi.org/mayer.htm
www.utne.com/azEQ.tmpl
www.queendom.com/cgi-bin/tests
www.nlp.com

Link to Useful Resources

www.universal-manager.co.uk

APPENDIX 3

NEBS Management Diploma in Management

NEBS Management is the Awarding Body for specialist management qualifications — committed to developing qualifications which meet the needs of today's managers at all levels across industry.

The NEBS Management Diploma in Management is a broad management development programme aimed at practising and aspiring middle managers. It offers a comprehensive, integrated programme of personal and organizational development.

Content

During the Diploma programme, a candidate will:

- Establish a Personal Development Plan
- Study theory and practice in the following key management areas:
  - Managing Human Resources
  - Financial Management
  - Organizational Activities and Change
  - Management Skills
- Produce a specialist Management Report
- Compile an Individual Development Portfolio.

Flexibility

The NEBS Management Diploma requires a minimum of 240 hours of study but can be completed on a full-time or part-time basis as appropriate. Many programmes will offer a mix of direct training, open learning and practical work-based activity. In connection with the Universal Manager series, the Diploma therefore offers the facility for learning in a variety of media including paper-based material, on-line resources and taught elements.

Assessment

Assessment of performance takes a rounded view of the capability demonstrated by the candidate in assignments and specialist tasks, in the management report and portfolio, and in interview.

Enrolment

The usual entry requirements are:

☞ At least two years' relevant management experience
☞ PLUS a NEBS Management Certificate, a Management S/NVQ at Level 3 or the equivalent qualification.

There are many Accredited Centres approved to offer the Diploma programme in the UK and abroad. Call NEBS Management on **020 7294 3053** for details of your nearest Centre.

INDEX